Three Progressives from Iowa

THE CENTER FOR THE STUDY OF THE RECENT HISTORY OF THE UNITED STATES

A cooperative undertaking involving

The State Historical Society of Iowa

The Herbert Hoover Presidential Library

and

The University of Iowa

THREE PROGRESSIVES FROM IOWA

GILBERT N. HAUGEN
HERBERT C. HOOVER
HENRY A. WALLACE

Edited by John N. Schacht

THE CENTER FOR THE STUDY OF THE
RECENT HISTORY OF THE UNITED STATES

IOWA CITY 1980

Library of Congress Cataloging in Publication Data
Main entry under title:

Three progressives from Iowa.

Papers presented at a conference held on Mar. 22, 1979, in Iowa City, under the sponsorship of the Center for the Study of the Recent History of the United States.
Includes bibliographical references.
1. Haugen, Gilbert Nelson, 1859-1933—Congresses. 2. Hoover, Herbert Clark, Pres. U.S., 1874-1964—Congresses. 3. Wallace, Henry Agard, 1888-1965—Congresses. 4. Progressivism (United States politics)—Congresses. 5. United States—Politics and government—20th century—Congresses. I. Schacht, John N., 1943- II. Center for the Study of the Recent History of the United States, Iowa City.

E747.T48   973.91'092'2   79-28845
ISBN 0-87414-013-7

CONTENTS

FOREWORD

THE PAPERS PRESENTED in this volume were delivered at a conference held on March 22, 1979, in Iowa City under the sponsorship of the Center for the Study of the Recent History of the United States, a cooperative undertaking involving the State Historical Society of Iowa, the Herbert Hoover Presidential Library, and The University of Iowa. Representatives of the three named institutions had been encouraged in the fall of 1975 by President Willard L. Boyd of The University to consider how they might work together to make a larger contribution to the study of the history of the United States in the twentieth century, and we decided that our efforts should focus at the outset on the resources for the study of recent American history available in the three libraries. This conclusion led to the publication in 1977 of *A Guide to the Resources*, which had been compiled by Boyd Keith Swigger under the direction of an advisory committee.

After a generous gift to help the proposed Center make a beginning had come from Mr. and Mrs. Clem T. Hanson of Moline, Illinois, the advisory committee, composed of Peter T. Harstad, director of the State Historical Society, Thomas T. Thalken, director of the Herbert Hoover Presidential Library, Lawrence Angove, executive director of the Herbert Hoover Presidential Library Association, Professors Lawrence E. Gelfand and Ellis W. Hawley of the university's history department, and the undersigned decided that the funds in hand should be used to conduct a conference on "Three Progressives from Iowa: Gilbert N. Haugen, Herbert C. Hoover, and Henry A. Wallace." Instructors of recent American history and closely related subjects in all of Iowa's colleges and universities and other residents of Iowa believed to have an interest in the purposes and potential of the Center were invited to the conference, and about 170 attended.

Additional funding for the projected conference on "Three Progressives from Iowa" came from the Procter and Gamble Fund of Cincinnati, Ohio, and this enabled the Center to plan for printing the three papers and the commentary delivered in an afternoon session and the single, longer paper presented in the evening. All five of the speakers, Professor Gilbert C. Fite of the University of Georgia, Professor Joan Hoff Wilson of Arizona State University, Professor Theodore A. Wilson of the University of Kansas, Professor Richard Lowitt of Iowa State University, and Professor Frank Freidel of Harvard University, had been requested to submit manuscripts which could be published in a separate volume, and their contributions were readied for the printer by John Schacht of the Reference Department in the University Libraries, who had completed other tasks relating to the conference.

The sincere thanks of the advisory committee go to Mr. and Mrs. Clem T. Hanson, to the Procter and Gamble Fund, to each of the five speakers, to John Schacht, and to the many others who helped to make a memorable and happy event of the first conference sponsored by the Center for the Study of the Recent History of the United States.

LESLIE W. DUNLAP
Dean of Library Administration and
Chairman of the Advisory Committee

October 11, 1979

Gilbert N. Haugen in 1912

GILBERT N. HAUGEN: PRAGMATIC PROGRESSIVE

GILBERT C. FITE

THE MIDDLE WEST provided a fertile environment for political progressivism in the early twentieth century. Iowa stood high among those states where Progressives contributed to political and economic change at both the state and national levels. While Gilbert N. Haugen, congressman from Iowa's Fourth District, did not become as well known as his fellow Iowans, Albert B. Cummins or Jonathan P. Dolliver, he was, nevertheless, an important figure in progressivism. If Haugen never became a household name in progressive circles before World War I, he did achieve national prominence as the sponsor of agricultural surplus control legislation in the 1920s. Of all matters before Congress between 1920 and the Great Depression, none overshadowed farm relief. The McNary-Haugen bills received almost constant congressional attention from 1924 to 1928. In working for progressive principles with emphasis upon helping farmers, Haugen earned the gratitude of Americans who believed in greater political and economic democracy.

Born on April 21, 1859, in Rock County, Wisconsin, Haugen was the son of Norwegian emigrants. Like many other young men in the post-Civil War years, he sought opportunities farther west. At age eighteen he bought a farm and settled in Worth County, Iowa. During the next few years, through hard work, careful management, and a keen sense for business, Haugen established a profitable economic base in northern Iowa. He acquired hundreds of acres of farm land, and also branched out into the implement, hardware, and other businesses. He moved to Northwood in 1887. In 1890 he and several other persons organized the Northwood Banking Company and established banks at Northwood and Kensett. Haugen became president of the company.

Accompanying his growing success as an entrepreneur was Haugen's desire for public service. Beginning in 1887, he held several local offices, and then won two terms in the Iowa legislature, where he served from 1894 to 1898. Out of

Gilbert C. Fite is Richard B. Russell Professor of History, University of Georgia. Professor Fite would like to acknowledge the help of his research assistant, Mr. Edward C. Nagy.

a deadlocked Republican convention in 1898, he obtained the nomination for Congress in the Fourth District. Stretching from Worth County in the west to the Mississippi River in the east, the Fourth District was a rich agricultural area covering ten counties where general farming, including dairying, predominated. The district had a population of about 169,000. Haugen won the election handily, polling 21,468 votes to 13,849 for his opponent, T. T. Blaise.[1] He took office on March 4, 1899. For the next thirty-four years, this farmer, banker, businessman, and politician served the people of his district without interruption.

Haugen's election to Congress coincided with a rising national demand for political and economic reform. An increasing number of Americans were demanding changes which would increase the influence of average citizens and reduce the power of special interests. Such programs as the initiative and referendum, the direct primary, and the direct election of senators were receiving growing support. Indeed, the first initiative and referendum law enacted by any state was passed by the South Dakota legislature in 1898, the year Haugen won election to the House. Complaints against business trusts and monopolies reached from the Atlantic to the Pacific. An increasing number of people were demanding more effective government regulation of the railroads and other business giants.

Upon arriving in Washington, Haugen had the good fortune of being a member of one of the most powerful state delegations in the nation's capital. Fellow Iowan David B. Henderson became the new Speaker of the House, and he appointed Haugen to the Committee on Agriculture. Because of his background and interests, Haugen found this assignment highly attractive. He believed with almost religious conviction that farmers were a special group of people upon whom the greatness of the country rested. To be a member of the Committee on Agriculture would place him in a position to serve those whom he considered the nation's most valuable citizens. Haugen held a position on the committee during his entire stay in Washington, and guided it as chairman from 1919 to 1931.

There was nothing in Haugen's background that would have predicted his later progressivism. Indeed, it might have been expected that his extensive business interests would have drawn him into the conservative ranks. But this was not the case. At least two factors bolstered his progressive stance. In the first place, philosophically Haugen was a democrat spelled with a small "d." He believed in the good sense of the average person and held that government should respond to citizen demands, hopes, and aspirations. Furthermore, he believed in economic opportunity for all. His fights were against laws and policies that restricted political or economic democracy. Secondly, Haugen was a keen politician, and he clearly recognized that the people of his district were becoming more progressive after the turn of the century. If he hoped to stay in office, he dared not run against that political current. But Haugen did not have to compromise his principles to stay in tune with the people of Iowa's Fourth District. The majority agreed with him and he with them.

One of the first major issues that commanded Haugen's attention as a new congressman was the sale of colored oleomargerine as a substitute for creamery butter. While southern cotton farmers may have benefited from the demand for cottonseed oil that went into the manufacture of oleo, midwestern dairy farmers resisted competition from the substitute product. In 1902 Haugen strongly supported the Grout bill, which raised the tax on colored oleo to ten cents a pound. It also prevented colored oleo produced in one state from being sold in any other state which prohibited its manufacture. Haugen claimed that additional legislation was needed to protect unwary consumers who might mistake colored oleo for butter. He argued that people must be protected from "wholesale fraud and deception." Haugen denied that the bill was designed to "ruin one industry for the benefit of another." It was, he said, simply a matter of insuring "purity and wholesomeness" and protecting "pure-butter producers against a fraudulent competition, as well as to protect the consumers." Furthermore, he urged his colleagues not to succumb to the agents of "unscrupulous corporations and individuals" who were palming off oleo on an unsuspecting public. Stand by the farmers, Haugen urged, and "I predict for you a place in the front ranks of those 5,000,000 dairymen in the grand march, passing through the pearly gates into a region where no oleomargerine is offered for sale."[2] While Haugen continued to be a guardian of the dairy farmers, even while attacking other special interests, he saw no contradiction in his position. He assumed that in working for the best interests of midwestern farmers he was defending the welfare of the entire nation.

By 1905 and 1906 a number of issues separating Progressives and conservatives were before Congress. These included stricter regulation of the railroads, which Haugen called one of the greatest questions "confronting the American people today;" pure food and drug legislation; and federal meat inspection.

In discussing the Hepburn bill, which called for increasing the powers of the Interstate Commerce Commission, Haugen said that railroads were setting rates at will and bleeding the people. High rates were established, he declared, "just to satisfy the greed, ambition, or need of a few operators on Wall Street to pay dividends on watered stock."[3] Haugen denied that he favored any attack on private property or wished to deprive the railroads of what was "fair and just." But he did insist that discrimination against farmers and other shippers must be eliminated. The desired political goal, he said, was legislation that would "promote happiness and give equal rights to all people."[4] Actually, he believed that the Hepburn bill did not go far enough toward effective regulation, but, as a practical Progressive, Haugen said the law could be improved later if it did not produce the desired results.[5]

Haugen favored the Meat Inspection Act of 1906 and fought for larger appropriations for the inspection program. He charged that the big packers, the beef trust, were trying to keep inspection funds so low that there would not be enough personnel to inspect the small packers and processors — who would then be unable to sell their meat abroad or in interstate commerce. The result, Haugen charged, would be "an absolute monopoly" for the large packers. Haugen recommended that if funds were indeed short, government salaries should be cut in order to employ more inspectors. Do not practice economy "altogether at the expense of agriculture," he pleaded.[6]

On the question of government regulation and anti-monopoly legislation, Haugen found himself lining up more and more with the progressive elements in Congress. He spoke frequently against monopoly and special privileges, often in the context of how farmers were hurt by industrial, transportation, and financial combinations. Theodore Roosevelt's trust-busting reputation received plaudits from Haugen. He referred to Roosevelt as "the most fearless, conscientious, resolute and well-meaning President that ever occupied that chair."[7] Haugen joined with those who believed new monetary legislation would bring major benefits to the average citizen. Calling for principles later incorporated in the Federal Reserve Act, he said in 1908 that the country needed "a currency available to move crops, an elastic currency; a currency that will expand and contract and that will adjust itself to existing conditions; a currency not in the interests of banks, nor for a few, but in the interest and benefit of all the people."[8]

But Haugen broke with many of his progressive colleagues when he came out against the parcel post system. He opposed parcel post on two grounds. His first objection centered around the advantage that parcel post would give to mail order houses at the expense of local merchants. It was the small town businessmen, Haugen argued, who paid the taxes and supported local government, schools, churches, and other community institutions. Rather than considering parcel post as an agency that could help consumers, he viewed it as something that would strengthen distant corporations. More important, however, was his vigorous objection to putting the federal government in "the freight or express business." Haugen had little faith in the efficiency of government business operations. He cited the Post Office and the Government Printing Office as examples of costly inefficiency. He saw future deficits if parcel post were established, deficits which would have to be covered by federal appropriations — and all in "the interest of catalogue houses."[9] Such a system, he claimed, would "build up an absolute monopoly in the mercantile business." Mentioning the beef and harvester trusts, Haugen said the country was already plagued with too many monopolies. He declared that he could not support a system that would destroy the merchants of those "beautiful towns" in order to "promote monopoly."[10]

In areas of regulation, Haugen was willing to extend government functions and powers in the best progressive tradition, but he had no faith in the federal government's ability to conduct business. He regularly referred to the high cost and inefficiency of government operations. "Excessive cost," he told his colleagues, "seems to be the result in everything the government undertakes to do."[11] Indeed, he had no patience with the growing federal bureaucracy nor with the increasing cost of government. He often criticized the failure of government business undertakings "due to red-tape, bunglesome and unbusiness like ways of transacting business founded on political and not business principles." He opposed postal savings, parcel post, and federal guarantee of bank deposits because, he said, they were "all steps in the direction of government ownership and socialism."[12]

The two issues that did most to divide the Republican party in 1909 and 1910 were the tariff and the fight over the powers of Speaker Joseph G. Cannon. Before those controversies were settled, Haugen was firmly in the camp of the party insurgents. As a true and loyal Republican, the party squabbles and division distressed him, but for Haugen principle was more important than party unity.

Like a number of other Progressives, Haugen thought that some tariff rates under the Dingley law of 1897 were too high. In the campaign of 1908 the Republicans had promised tariff revision, which to Haugen and many others meant revising rates downward. However, he believed in the protective tariff principle and often associated America's phenomenal economic growth with protection. What concerned him was whether farmers were benefiting from tariff duties and whether some rates were contributing to business monopoly. When the tariff came up for discussion in 1908 and 1909, Haugen argued that in general rates should be lowered and on some iron and lumber products entirely removed.[13] While Haugen favored reducing tariff duties on some iron products that might result in lower prices for wire and other items sold to his farmer constituents, he vigorously supported the home market argument. He claimed that a thriving industrial economy protected by tariff duties could pay good wages, which in turn meant a strong demand for agricultural products.

As the Payne-Aldrich bill moved toward passage in 1909, Haugen resented the strict control which Speaker Cannon and other high tariff advocates maintained over the legislative process. He wanted a separate vote on the rates for several items, but the party leadership would not permit it except on four or five commodities. Consequently, Haugen voted against the conference report, hoping that the bill would be forced back to conference where it could be revised and improved.[14] Haugen did not consider his action disloyal to the Republican party because he believed that he was more in line with the 1908 party platform than the high tariff faction of the party. Anyway, he said, his first loyalties were to the people's welfare and not to the party bosses.

During debate over tariff legislation, the arbitrary power exerted by Speaker Cannon in the House aroused increasing resentment. In February, 1909, Haugen was one of twenty-nine insurgent Republicans who introduced a resolution to amend the House rules to reduce the Speaker's control.[15] He wrote former governor William Larrabee that "for some time" he had favored changing the rules so there would be a more "equitable distribution of the power."[16] He later told another Iowan that there must be more legislation for the people "and less for special interests." One way to achieve that goal was to permit representatives in Washington to vote their own consciences and the desires of their constituents.[17]

By early 1910 a strong move was under way to challenge Speaker Cannon. Haugen put out a statement explaining that the "insurgent" movement was designed to revise the "arbitrary rules" and to restore "the principle of representative government."[18] He wrote on January 17 that the insurgents would "continue to hand it out to Uncle Joe on the installment plan." Haugen's resentment boiled at the expectation by Cannon that members of the House would subordinate their freedom, independence, and the interest of their constituents to those of the czarist Speaker.[19] In March, 1910, Haugen backed his colleague, George W. Norris of Nebraska, who led a successful showdown fight against Cannon. Haugen denied that the insurgents were opposing Republican principles or the party platform. So far as he was concerned, he explained, the only objective was to amend the rules so that members of the House could "assert their rights."[20]

Scores of people from Haugen's home district praised him for his stand on the speakership fight and his progressive stance on other issues. However, he aroused the opposition of conservatives, or "stalwarts," who were determined to defeat him for reelection in 1910.[21] Critics charged that Haugen and other Progressives had embarrassed President Taft and were hurting the party. Haugen, however, insisted that he was supporting Taft just as he had Roosevelt. He said that he believed Taft was honest and trying to do the right thing, although differences over issues did exist.[22] But the Republican split between Progressives and conservatives, and rising Democratic strength, were of real concern to Haugen as he sought his seventh term in the House. One supporter wrote him that the "standpat" Republicans and conservative Democrats were trying to defeat him with "the lavish use of money."[23] The best efforts of Haugen's opponents, however, could not defeat him, and he won reelection by a narrow margin of 220 votes. Nevertheless, the Democrats took control of the House of Representatives, and Haugen became a minority member of the Committee on Agriculture, where he had worked so hard for the farm interests.

By 1910 Haugen had fully established his progressive credentials. He had not favored every reform or policy advocated by persons calling themselves progressive, but he had been what might be called a discriminating Progressive who had supported those causes which would in his view best serve the people, especially farmers. He had a strong record on railroad rate regulation, meat inspection, expansion of rural free delivery, moderating the protective tariff rates, and supporting enlargement of the functions of the Department of

Agriculture. He had fought for measures which he believed would curb the special interests and strengthen economic equality and opportunity. Yet in 1912 Haugen refused to support Theodore Roosevelt and the Progressive party against Taft. He had been nominated by the regular Republican organization and he did not consider voting for Roosevelt to be the test of progressive orthodoxy. Haugen wrote that he would stand on his own progressive record.[24]

During the years between 1911 and 1919, when the Democrats controlled the House of Representatives, Congress passed a substantial amount of legislation that vitally affected farmers. These laws included the Federal Farm Loan Act, the Federal Warehouse Act, and the Rural Post Roads Act, all of 1916, and the Smith-Lever and the Smith-Hughes Acts of 1914 and 1917, which provided federal assistance for agricultural education. Although they were sponsored by Democratic leaders, Haugen gave these and other measures active support. During the Democratic interlude, Haugen was the leading minority member in the House Agriculture Committee. The Republican victory in 1918 at last elevated him to the committee chairmanship in the first session of the Sixty-sixth Congress, in May 1919.

Within a year after Haugen assumed the top post in the House Agriculture Committee, farm prices began their sharp postwar drop. This was a shock to farmers, who had enjoyed better than usual times for nearly twenty years, and their spokesmen in Washington were as uncertain as the farmers at home in regard to what should be done. But everyone in the agricultural sector recognized the problem. Prices for wheat, cotton, livestock, and other farm commodities began to drop in the middle of 1920, and by 1921 agriculture was experiencing a severe recession, if not a full scale depression. Net farm income to operators dropped from $8.7 to $3.3 billion between 1919 and 1921. Those farmers who had bought high-priced land on credit during World War I or who had increased their debt for other purposes found themselves in a tenuous position. Farmers were especially hard hit because non-farm prices did not fall in proportion to those of farm commodities. This created a keen disparity between farmers and other elements in the economy. If the price index in 1913 is considered as 100, the purchasing power of several major farm products had dropped to 67 by 1921. Suffering from a critical cost-price squeeze, thousands of farmers went broke in 1921 and 1922.[25]

Both real and self-styled friends of farmers advanced a wide range of proposals to solve what was rapidly being dubbed the "farm problem." Some advocated more credit for farmers, others urged the federal government to set agricultural prices at a profitable level to producers, and there was some support for export subsidies and aid to cooperative marketing. There was even a small inflationist group, which suggested expanding the currency in the greenback-free silver tradition.[26]

While many of his colleagues in 1920 and 1921 were filling the *Congressional Record* with speeches on the difficulties confronting farmers, Haugen concentrated on his work as committee chairman. The House Committee on Agriculture was one of the most heavily worked bodies in Congress during those immediate postwar years. Haugen held 111 days of hearings in the Sixty-sixth Congress (1919-1921) alone. The committee considered measures ranging from legislation to help eradicate the pink bollworm in the Cotton South to the regulation of packers and stockyards. Speaking early in 1922, Haugen said that since 1919 Congress had amended more old laws and passed more new legislation on behalf of agriculture than in any similar period since he had arrived in Washington more than twenty years earlier.[27] Haugen considered passage of the Packers and Stockyards Act, which he sponsored, as one of his major achievements. He also considered the Tincher law, regulating the trading in grain futures, as highly important. In 1922 Congress passed the Capper-Volstead Act, which, under most circumstances, exempts farmer cooperatives from antitrust action, and the next year lawmakers enacted the Intermediate Credits Act to provide additional farm credit. However, regulatory and credit legislation did not get at the heart of the farm problem, which was disparity between the prices of farm and nonfarm commodities.

While Congress wrestled with ways and means to alleviate ills on the farm, a small group of businessmen, officials in the United States Department of Agriculture, a few farm organization leaders, and others were working toward a new approach to America's farm problems. Foremost among this group was George N. Peek, president of the Moline Plow Company from 1919 to 1924. By late 1921 Peek and his associate, Hugh Johnson, had developed a farm relief plan which they called "equality for agriculture." Surpluses were what tended to drive prices down. Therefore, Peek and Johnson came up with the idea of segregating the surpluses of basic crops and letting the price of the domestically consumed portion rise behind a tariff wall, or to a price that would give the product the same purchasing power that it had in the prewar period from 1905 to 1914. The surplus part of the crop would be sold abroad at the world price. The Peek-Johnson plan would be administered by an agricultural export corporation, which would sell the price-depressing surpluses abroad. Losses incurred on overseas sales would be recouped by placing a tax, called an equalization fee, on each bushel or unit of the commodity sold by producers. This, it was argued, would provide a fund to cover any export losses but still leave the producer with an increased income.[28]

A bill based on these principles was prepared in the fall and early winter of 1923. There is no evidence that Haugen had any part in framing the legislation, but he liked the concept of equality incorporated in the plan. As chairman of the House Agriculture Committee, he introduced the measure in the House on January 16, 1924, and Senator Charles L. McNary presented it to the Senate. It is doubtful if Haugen realized that he had attached his name to a bill that would earn him such a prominent and lasting place in the history of twentieth-century agriculture and farm policy.

Nevertheless, Haugen was firmly convinced that the traditional remedies advanced to help farmers — inflation, credit, cooperatives, and regulation of big business — were inadequate to meet current conditions facing farmers. In conducting hearings on the bill, he made sure that the unfavorable circumstances among producers were properly aired. He sent hundreds of copies of the printed hearings to supporters who used them for educational and propaganda purposes. The testimony presented a grim picture of agricultural conditions. On April 24 Haugen's committee voted out the McNary-Haugen bill by a vote of 14 to 6.[29] In the fifteen hours allocated for House debate on the first McNary-Haugen bill, Haugen arranged one-fourth of the time for himself.[30]

Like a good many other farm spokesmen, Haugen believed that the farmers' main problem was, as he put it, "this inequality in prices between agricultural commodities and other commodities." He held that this inequality prevented farmers from getting adequate returns on their labor and capital. On May 20, after explaining the bill's provisions to his colleagues and discussing how the McNary-Haugen measure would give farmers equality in the economy, Haugen launched into a lengthy discussion of the legislation.

Haugen advanced several major arguments on behalf of his bill. First, he insisted that farmers as individuals were at a disadvantage in dealing with organized groups in the economy. The efforts of agriculturalists to organize, he said, had been unsuccessful, but the McNary-Haugen bill would give them the means to unite and increase their bargaining power. When critics argued that such power in the hands of farmers would increase consumer prices and the cost of living, Haugen made no apologies. Admitting that consumer prices might rise slightly, he expressed resentment at the idea that "consumers should get foodstuffs at less than cost of production to the ruin of American farming." Harking back to his discussion of reform legislation before 1910, he demanded "economic justice" and the sharing of social and economic benefits among "all classes of the people." In his discussion of any public issue, Haugen always seemed to return to the theme of fairness, equality of treatment, economic justice, and the old Theodore Roosevelt concept of a square deal.

Haugen's basic economic argument for farm relief centered in his belief that without a prosperous agriculture the nation could not for long enjoy good times. Many Americans held this view, but few could state it with more clarity and intensity than Haugen. He always referred to agriculture as "our basic industry," upon which all other economic activity rested. The "prosperity and happiness of our people depend upon the success of the tillers of the soil," he repeated time and again. No subject so stirred Haugen's soul and led him to such flights of oratory as a discussion of agricultural fundamentalism. In debating McNary-Haugenism, he said: "Just as sure as the sun rises in the East and sets in the West, without prosperity in agriculture our factories and mills and our banks would crumble to pieces. Our railroads would rust from idleness, our beautiful towns, villages, and cities, including our schoolhouses in the valleys and churches on the hilltops, would to a large extent suffer. Our grand and glorious government, its splendid and magnificent institutions would materially suffer." William Jennings Bryan could hardly have said it better.[31]

Neither reason nor emotional arguments about the importance of agriculture could convince members of the House of Representatives to pass the McNary-Haugen bill. Opponents charged that it was economically unsound, radical — even bolshevistic — unworkable, and a threat to the low cost of living. It was defeated by a vote of 223 to 155 on June 3. Haugen wrote that he was "very much disappointed" at the bill's defeat. He said that the measure had good support in the Middle West and Far West, except in the cities "where the Big-Five packers and grain exchanges are located." Passage of the measure by Congress, he wrote, would have helped business and labor, as well as farmers.[32]

During 1925 and 1926 there was a good deal of jockeying for legislative position among supporters of various kinds of farm relief. The Coolidge administration pushed for a cooperative marketing bill and opposed any legislation based on the McNary-Haugen principles. While Haugen was willing to report a bill to encourage cooperative marketing, he did not consider it "real [farm] relief legislation." The farm lobby, organized by George Peek, was sometimes at odds with Haugen and the Committee on Agriculture. Furthermore, it did not appear that any really helpful legislation could be passed without southern support. Cotton representatives opposed levying the equalization fee on cotton.

Haugen sometimes became annoyed at Peek and other farm lobbyists. He believed that they did not always act responsibly in their relations with himself and other legislative leaders. Haugen also had a suspicion that Peek was knowingly or unknowingly advancing Democratic interests in the Midwest. There were occasional differences between the non-congressional farm lobby and Haugen, and among congressional Republicans.[33]

Despite some genuine problems in moving the McNary-Haugen bill through Congress, the Senate passed the measure on February 11, 1927, and Haugen steered the House to a favorable vote six days later. It had taken pressure, patience, and compromise to finally achieve victory. While the 1927 bill was somewhat different from that voted on in 1924, it still contained the equalization fee, which Haugen thought was the "heart and soul" of the legislation. It was well known that President Coolidge disapproved the McNary-Haugen bill, and no one was surprised when he vetoed the measure. While Haugen had thought at one time that "we shall be able to pass the bill over the President's veto," that was a misjudgment.[34]

Following adjournment of Congress in 1927, Haugen traveled around his district and elsewhere, talking up his brand of farm relief. Back in Washington late in the year, the agricultural forces organized to pass another McNary-Haugen bill. Haugen's committee reported the measure by a vote of

15 to 6 on March 26, but a bitter battle ensued over whether to eliminate or retain the equalization fee. At the insistence of Haugen and others the fee was retained, and both houses passed the bill in the spring of 1928.[35] But the fight over the fee proved anticlimactic, as Coolidge again killed the legislation with a stinging veto.

Meanwhile, Peek and some other Republicans were talking about bolting the Republican party in the forthcoming presidential race if the GOP did not nominate a person friendly to McNary-Haugen principles. Haugen hoped that one or both major parties would nominate a man who was pledged to "real farm relief," but he had no intention of deserting his party on the farm issue. He personally favored Frank O. Lowden, former governor of Illinois and friend of surplus-control legislation, but when Herbert Hoover received the nomination Haugen announced his support for the ticket. Despite Hoover's strong opposition to Haugen's brand of farm relief, Haugen, as a loyal Republican, participated in a homecoming program for Hoover at West Branch in August, 1928.[36] While disagreeing with Hoover on the equalization fee, Haugen said he admired his "honest convictions," "many achievements," "long experience," "great ability," and "high type of character, founded upon integrity."[37] Haugen agreed with Congressman Lester J. Dickinson of Algona, who wrote that it would be a "catastrophe" for farmers of the Midwest "to turn their interests over to Al Smith who represents the consumers of New York."[38]

During the campaign, Hoover had promised agricultural relief through government support to farmer cooperatives. Haugen had little faith in this solution, but he recognized the futility of bucking the president on this issue. Thus, as chairman of the House Agriculture Committee, he reported out the Agricultural Marketing bill supported by Hoover. He voted for it, but without enthusiasm. Haugen said that the law might do some good, but his statements lacked any genuine conviction.[39] The Agricultural Marketing Act proved to be the failure that many of its early critics predicted.

In 1930 the Democrats returned to power in the House, and in 1931 Haugen lost his chairmanship of the Agriculture Committee. The welfare of farmers, nevertheless, continued to be a major interest until he was defeated for reelection in the Democratic landslide of 1932. He died in July, 1933, after being sick for several months. As Haugen lay ill in the spring of 1933, Congress passed the Agricultural Adjustment Act to restore farm purchasing power, an objective for which Haugen had worked at least a dozen years. The new direction of farm policy had its roots in McNary-Haugenism, and in this respect Haugen and his associates in the 1920s had paved the way for what they had called "real farm relief."

Gilbert N. Haugen served his constituents in Iowa's Fourth District for thirty-four years. His main contribution to Iowans and to the nation was his work on behalf of farmers. He held firmly to the proposition that agriculture was the most valuable industry; it followed that he considered farmers to be the nation's most useful citizens. According to Haugen, their welfare was basic to the strength, progress, and happiness of America. Thus, for more than a third of a century, he opposed policies and principles which he believed were harmful to farmers and supported those which he thought would be helpful. Between the time he went to Washington in 1899 and his death some thirty-four years later, federal appropriations and services to agriculture had increased phenomenally. Haugen was very much a part of the forces that brought about that development.

Gilbert N. Haugen was not one of the nation's leading Progressives. Nevertheless, his support for practical progressive and reform causes place him among the significant political figures of the early twentieth century. He was a leader who saw the changing problems arising from industrialism and the growth of big business. Haugen favored a modest expansion of governmental powers to protect the weak, to assure equal opportunity, to reduce economic exploitation, and to guarantee fair treatment to all. The declining bargaining position of individual farmers in an increasingly organized economy was a special concern to him.

Haugen's progressivism was based on a practical approach to problems and the development of specific remedies to deal with them. His actions were not motivated by any firmly held ideology other than his agrarian fundamentalism. While favoring the expansion of government functions and powers for some purposes, he had serious doubts about the efficiency of government administration. Long before Jimmy Carter, Haugen sharply criticized government inefficiency, the unresponsiveness of bureaucrats to people's needs, and the growing cost of government.

Haugen will not be remembered as a great political leader in the usual meaning of that term. On the other hand, he was a cut or two above many of his colleagues in the House. He was an important figure among that second level of leadership in Congress, which furnished much of the good sense, practical wisdom, and political know-how on which the strength of American democracy rested.

NOTES

1　*Congressional Directory* (Washington: Government Printing Office, 1899), 29. For a full account of Haugen's early career, see the manuscript biography by Peter T. Harstad and Bonnie Michael, Iowa State Historical Department, Division of the State Historical Society, Iowa City (in the authors' possession).

2　U.S. Congress, House, 57th Cong., 1st sess., Feb. 10, 1902, *Congressional Record*, 1530-43. In 1900 Congressman William W. Grout of Vermont introduced a bill to place a ten cents a pound tax on colored oleo and making it illegal to sell the colored product in states that prohibited such sales. When a major drive finally began to remove the discriminatory tax on oleo in the late 1940s, no less a liberal than Hubert H. Humphrey led the unsuccessful campaign to retain the tax in the interest of creamery butter. R. Alton Lee, *A History of Regulatory Taxation* (Lexington, Ky., 1973), 48-53, 58.

3 U.S. Congress, House, 58th Cong., 3rd sess., Feb. 9, 1905, *Congressional Record*, A187.

4 *Ibid.*, 59th Cong., 1st sess., Feb. 6, 1906, 2171-74.

5 *Ibid.*, 58th Cong., 3rd sess., Feb. 9, 1905, A187.

6 *Ibid.*, 59th Cong., 1st sess., Jan. 26, 1906, 1618-19, and June 23, 1906, A121ff.

7 *Ibid.*, 60th Cong., 1st sess., March 24, 1908, 3835.

8 *Ibid.*, May 14, 1908, A153-54.

9 *Ibid.*, 59th Cong., 1st sess., March 7, 1906, 3480.

10 *Ibid.*

11 *Ibid.*, 3481.

12 *Ibid.*, 60th Cong., 1st sess., March 13, 1908, 3291; Gilbert N. Haugen to J. E. Stinehart, Feb. 6, 1909, Gilbert N. Haugen Papers, Iowa State Historical Department, Division of the State Historical Society, Iowa City. There is a guide to the Haugen Papers prepared by Bonnie Michael. All Haugen correspondence cited hereafter is found in the Haugen Papers.

13 U.S. Congress, House, 60th Cong., 1st sess., May 18, 1908, *Congressional Record*, 6490.

14 Haugen to P. P. Cole, May 9, 1910, and to L. H. Henry, May 23, 1910.

15 U.S. Congress, House, 60th Cong., 2nd sess., Feb. 9, 1909, *Congressional Record*, 2116.

16 Haugen to William Larrabee, Feb. 22, 1909.

17 Haugen to H. Engebretson, Jan. 19, 1910.

18 Undated statement, 1910, Haugen Papers.

19 U.S. Congress, House, 61st Cong., 2nd sess., June 17, 1910, *Congressional Record*, 8421.

20 Haugen to Henry, May 23, 1910.

21 Haugen to V. L. Gilje, May 15, 1910.

22 Haugen to Cole, May 9, 1910.

23 Undated letter to Haugen (writer's signature unclear), 1910; and C. F. Chambers to Haugen, Nov. 9, 1910.

24 Wiley S. Rankin to Haugen, Aug. 13, 1912, and Haugen to Rankin, Aug. 17, 1912. Several of Haugen's political supporters urged him to support Roosevelt.

25 See Gilbert C. Fite, *George N. Peek and the Fight for Farm Parity* (Norman, Ok., 1954), chap. I, and Henry C. Wallace's "Report of the Secretary," in *Yearbook of Agriculture* (Washington: Government Printing Office, 1923), 1-35.

26 Fite, 13-19. The best study on the inflation movement is David D. Webb, "Farmers, Professors and Money: Agriculture and the Battle for Managed Money, 1920-1941" (Ph.D. dissertation, University of Oklahoma, 1978).

27 U.S. Congress, House, 67th Cong., 2nd sess., March 23, 1922, *Congressional Record*, 4478-79.

28   Fite, chaps. III and IV.

29   Haugen to L. G. Hewitt, April 24, 1924; to S. E. Elliott, April 17, 1924; and to Director of the Minnesota Farm Bureau Federation, Feb. 26, 1924. See also Fite, 59.

30   U.S. Congress, House, 68th Cong., 1st sess., May 20, 1924, *Congressional Record*, 9021ff.

31   *Ibid.*, 9032.

32   Haugen to E. N. Haugen, June 7, 1924, and to H. O. Myran, Aug. 15, 1924.

33   U.S. Congress, House, 68th Cong., 2nd sess., Feb. 25, 1925, *Congressional Record*, 4671-72; *ibid.*, 69th Cong., 1st sess., April 26, 1926, 8236. See also Harstad and Michael, manuscript biography of Haugen, chap. XII.

34   Haugen to L. P. Barth, April 18, 1927.

35   The Senate passed the bill in early April and the House passed it on May 3. Haugen to K. A. Kleppe, March 27, 1928, and to Helen Taylor, May 3, 1928.

36   Haugen to A. W. Ricker, Feb. 9, 1928; to J. W. Sandusky, Feb. 14, 1928; to Wil V. Tufford, May 31, 1928, and to F. L. Pearson, Aug. 16, 1928. Haugen was at first reluctant to announce his support of Hoover, but eventually he made his position clear enough.

37   Haugen to W. Earl Hall, Sept. 28, 1928.

38   L. J. Dickinson to Haugen, Aug. 9, 1928; Haugen to T. H. Megorden, Sept. 29, 1928; to F. Z. Nichols, Sept. 21, 1928; and to Frank K. Nies, Aug. 20, 1928.

39   Haugen to R. B. Bergeson, April 25, 1929; to Carl Williams, June 6, 1929; and to Melchr Luchsinger, Aug. 19, 1929.

Herbert C. Hoover in 1938

HERBERT HOOVER'S PROGRESSIVE RESPONSE TO THE NEW DEAL

JOAN HOFF WILSON

HERBERT HOOVER DIFFERS from the other men under consideration at this conference in three basic ways. First, his progressivisim, unlike theirs, has often been denied and continues to be subjected to critical scrutiny. Second, some of the suspicion about his progressive credentials arises from the fact that he never enjoyed widespread support from either the farm bloc in Congress or from rank and file farmers in the 1920s and early thirties. Third, at no time in his long public career as secretary of commerce, president of the United States, and later as self-appointed critic of the New Deal, did he ever concentrate primarily on agricultural matters. Agriculture constituted but one component of his comprehensive economic plans for the nation and the world.[1]

From recent reviews of David Burner's new biography of Hoover, one can only conclude that his progressivism remains a hotly contested issue among certain historians.[2] I cannot presume to settle this debate today, but I feel obliged to enter into the fray one more time by commenting upon Hoover's progressivism before turning to certain aspects of his critique of the New Deal between 1933 and 1935. In fact, it is only in light of his very particular and identifiable brand of progressivism that his initial criticisms of the depression policies of FDR can be fully understood.

Had progressivism been a less multifaceted movement, perhaps Hoover could logically be excluded from its ranks. But it was not. Both before and after World War I, the American Progressive movement encompassed almost every imaginable kind of social reformer. Only avowed Socialists, Communists, Syndicalists, and Fascists did not fall well within its amorphous parameters. Prior to 1914, moralistic and scientific arguments had joined forces in an attempt to solve the psychological and physical problems created by

Joan Hoff Wilson is Professor of History, Arizona State University. Professor Wilson wishes to thank Ruth Dennis, Mildred Mather, and Robert Wood for their cooperation in conducting "long distance" research on this topic at the Herbert Hoover Presidential Library.

industrialization. As a result, very diverse groups coalesced in a search for a more efficient socioeconomic order based on bureaucratic and technological innovations that would not totally obviate traditional political standards and social mores.[3]

This unstable mixture of potentially contradictory elements became most apparent in those Progressives who, like Hoover, concentrated on rationalizing the political economy of the United States and aiding the victims of industrialization with modern technological methods while continuing to cling to basically nineteenth-century agrarian ideals about morality and the role of the individual in the democratic process. Only a small group of so-called "perfect" Progressives, according to Otis Graham, managed to achieve "just the right vision and balance," by taking "from the moralists their passion for risky, worthy causes, and from the scientists their mental flexibility and their respect for technical expertise in the service of the public." (Curiously, most of Graham's "perfect" Progressives came from the social welfare ranks of the movement.)[4]

No reformer in search of a new order could occupy this delicately balanced position for long. Hoover walked the progressive tightrope of perfection most successfully in the 1920s as secretary of commerce. Although he inevitably fell off, it is possible in retrospect to recognize that at its functional best his social engineering brand of progressivism represented the middle course between that of the farsighted but often insensitive scientists and the well-intentioned but shortsighted moralists. It is not surprising that, in retrospect, progressivism often appeared as a well-intentioned, if frantic, uncoordinated, and sometimes counterproductive movement. Its adherents were attempting the impossible: to produce more democracy and more efficiency while preserving individualism and increasing cooperation. However, for a brief period before and after World War I, the rubric of efficiency effectively eclipsed the paradoxical aspects of progressivism. All reformers, whether motivated by self-interest or altruism, by science or morality, by urban or rural prejudices, responded to the call to eliminate waste and suffering and to improve societal conditions through efficient organization.

As an engineer Hoover proved particularly susceptible to a movement permeated by concepts of efficiency. The same scientific and moral justifications of efficiency which characterized progressivism had their counterparts in the engineering profession. By the First World War one group of American engineers came under the direct influence of the scientific management ideas of Frederick Winslow Taylor, an engineer who specialized in developing efficiency techniques for industry which could be applied to all social activities and institutions. Although most engineers prided themselves "on being hard-headed practical men," the Taylorites in particular emphasized analysis of statistical data and cause and effect relationships. Hoover agreed with Taylor that theoretically there was a common interest between employer and employee, but that this natural, mutual harmony of interests in society had all but been eradicated by monopoly growth. They further agreed that harmonious relationships could only be restored by a mental and structural revolution under the leadership of scientifically oriented engineers. This was social control progressivism. Its advocates were dedicated to reorganizing and coordinating governmental and economic functions through centralization, simplification, and statistical research.[5]

To accomplish such a feat would have required a basic value change in American society and the restructuring of capitalism. This in turn would have necessitated the formulation of a comprehensive, modern ideology for America. Hoover was one of the few disciples of Taylor who perceived the political as well as the technological magnitude of the task of reorganizing modern society along efficient lines. His later theoretical writings clearly indicate that, unlike many social control engineers, he did not accept centralization as the most efficient or democratic economy of scale to insure a humane, technocratic future. Technology, according to Hoover, could bring the material benefits of modern society within the reach of all Americans only if they retained a sense of community consciousness and decentralized organizations in their pursuit of a better life.[6]

Another group of engineers approached the question of social responsibility primarily from a moralistic point of view. They also believed in progress through technology, but wanted to make sure that free enterprise, individual initiative, and equality of opportunity survived in any improved society of the future. Placing greater stress upon *a priori* ethical judgments associated with individualism and the philosophy of material success through hard work, they usually defended traditional American capitalism against attacks from the left, especially those coming from organized labor. While believing that moral and technological progress was "written into the laws of the universe," they did not want progress at the expense of the American way of life — what Hoover later called "the American system." During such crises as war or depression, they usually defended the *status quo*. At the very most, they stood for more of the same, with minor legislative modifications of economic and political institutions, recognizing the engineer's special ability to make society function more smoothly.[7]

Unlike many of his more moralistically oriented engineering colleagues, Hoover did not uncritically accept the traditional American values of uncontrolled individualism and materialism. Instead, he tried to temper the legacy of nineteenth-century materialistic individualism by advocating a sense of social responsibility and voluntary cooperation. He saw the problem as one of preserving the necessary amount of competition and initiative in the daily economic lives and experiences of Americans while maintaining equality of opportunity and coordinating numerous individual efforts for the collective benefit of all. He finally rejected any form of forced bureaucratization or national regimentation of the economy as "false liberalism" because it destroyed the minimum individual incentive and confidence he believed necessary to preserve the best of American democracy and capitalism.[8]

Hoover could identify comfortably with each of the two major schools of engineering thought because their *differences* often reflected unconscious or unexamined private assumptions, while their *similarities* constituted publicly acknowledged unifying principles. Although both groups *publicly* united behind the need for greater rationalization of the political economy, they did not always *privately* agree on the value of centralization in politics or economics. To many Taylorites, regimentation of the political economy was inherently inefficient and hence ineffective. Most moralists viewed arbitrary restrictions on individual actions as not only evil but also unconstitutional. Subtle shifts of emphasis placed an engineer in one camp or the other — sometimes more on the side of collective efficiency, sometimes more on the side of individual liberty, and sometimes indiscriminately on both sides of the question. Very often this emphasis changed periodically in the career of a single individual. Such was the case with Hoover.

Given the variations of progressivism among engineers, let alone among other professional groups and the public at large, it is much too simplistic to argue, as Arthur M. Schlesinger, Jr. recently has, that the "real" Progressives of Hoover's time were exclusively those who sought "national control of business and natural resources in the public interest." Clearly it is New Deal hindsight (or dogmatism) carried to its logical extreme when only reformers like George W. Norris, Robert M. LaFollette, Jr., Fiorello LaGuardia, Gifford Pinchot, Harold Ickes, and Henry A. Wallace deserve the title of Progressive Republicans.[9]

While Schlesinger may exclude Hoover from the ranks of Progressivism, Hoover did not exclude himself. From the very beginning of his political career, following World War I, he thought of himself as an independent Progressive. This meant that he neither identified with the Old Guard Republicans to his right or with the more radical, largely agrarian wing of the GOP to his left. As early as February, 1920, before he entered the race for the Republican presidential nomination, Hoover met with Colonel Edward M. House and other Democratic leaders. At that time House still considered Hoover a possible nominee of the Democrats. After revealing his Republican background to the Colonel, Hoover said that he wanted to try to "liberalize" Republicans and "perhaps force them into the kind of Progressive party that [Theodore] Roosevelt at one time had in mind, but which he abandoned in Chicago in 1916." He confided to House that "if Roosevelt had not surrendered then and had kept the Progressive Party together that he [Hoover] . . . could get the Progressive nomination and sweep the country." His identification with TR's progressivism was belatedly borne out in a 1965 quantitative analysis of the 1912 election in Iowa which indicated that had Hoover been living and voting in his home state he would have exhibited all the characteristics of a "Bull Moose" Republican.[10]

To those who knew Hoover best, it came as no surprise when he issued a public letter on March 8, 1920, describing himself as an independent Progressive who thought that the serious postwar problems confronting the country should transcend partisanship. After his short-lived 1920 candidacy for the Republican nomination ended, Hoover wrote to Robert A. Taft about his perceptions of himself and the future direction of the party. He expressed the disappointment of the "independent and progressive Republicans" like himself over aspects of the platform and other results of the Chicago nominating convention. He wanted the progressive Republicans, whom he referred to as the "liberal thinkers of the party" and whom he believed represented the majority in 1920, to unite against conservative legislative actions on the state and federal level.[11] Throughout the 1920s Hoover continued to think that his actions consistently reflected the views of these middle-of-the-road progressive Republicans, although some, like Mark Sullivan, thought that his ideas on taxes, for example, were too far to the left of center.[12]

The fact that fewer nationally recognized Progressives supported him for the presidency in 1928 than had supported him in 1920, and that six out of the twelve agrarian Republican senators who identified themselves as Progressives actively opposed his candidacy in 1932, is not conclusive proof that Hoover had abandoned his own tenets of social engineering progressivism. In 1928 and 1932 neither presidential candidate of the two major parties received the support of a majority of the remaining Progressives across the country because the movement had fragmented into so many different factions. Nonetheless, a small private poll of social workers showed two-thirds favored Hoover in 1928, and some "perfect" social welfare Progressives like Jane Addams stayed with him in 1932.[13]

Even after his defeat for the presidency in 1932, Hoover and his closest advisers continued to talk about organizing a liberal or progressive nucleus within the party, drawing from young, less radical (and less conservative) GOP members. Hoover ruefully admitted to an Iowa editor in May, 1933, that his problem with members of his own party was that he had always been "too progressive," but that extreme political reactions to the New Deal made the search for a rational, moderate progressive candidate to lead the Republican party all the more imperative. Ironically, in 1933, 1934, and 1935, he and his friends came close to agreeing on only one man — Frank Knox, the Chicago publisher, who became Alf Landon's pugnacious running mate in 1936.[14]

This review of the engineering characteristics of Hoover's progressivism and his own, as well as others', perception of him as a progressive leader clears the way for me to discuss the subtleties of his response to the New Deal. The title of the paper has a double meaning. First, it implies that on the basis of his previous career as a Progressive, Hoover's comments on the New Deal have been unfairly and often unthinkingly labeled reactionary. After all, George Wolfskill, Leonard P. Liggio, Ronald Radosh, and other students of critics of the New Deal have documented that the ultraconservative Republican opponents of FDR — the leaders of big business and banking interests, especially those who had been members of the Liberty League — retired from the battle during the mid-1930s, after they discovered they had little to fear from the New Deal's melange of reformism. Thus moderate Republicans and leftover GOP Progressives like Hoover composed the bulk of the so-called Old Right anti-New Dealers by 1940. In addition, when Hoover's background is quantitatively compared to that of Progressives such as those studied by Graham in *Encore for Reform,* it is easy to see that he shares a statistically reliable range of similar characteristics with them.[15]

The second meaning of the title suggests the idea that there was some kind of change or shift in Hoover's critique of the New Deal. By the fall of 1934, the emphasis in his response turned from the pragmatic, statistical approach he had demonstrated so ably when secretary of commerce to an emotional condemnation of the New Deal as a violation of traditional American institutions and liberty. The paradoxical mixture of science and moralism which plagued so many Progressives, and which Hoover had seemingly balanced so well in the 1920s, deserted him within a relatively short time after he left office as a defeated depression president.

Only twice in his life did Hoover forsake his strong belief that progress occurred primarily through applied science and technology. National traumas triggered both shifts in emphasis, and in each case he resorted to writing about a moralistic view of progress based on the ideals of individualism and liberty. His first retreat to progressive moralism occurred in the wake of World War I, when he published *American Individualism* in 1922. Important as an early indication of the socioeconomic parameters of his thinking, this small book contained vague arguments and unclearly defined terms that often left readers confused and uncertain about how he planned to draw upon the best aspects of America's individualistic heritage to create a decentralized corporate society. Fortuitously, his impressive managerial activities as secretary of commerce quickly overshadowed the obvious ambiguities in his own thinking. The public soon forgot the ideas in *American Individualism* until several generations later, when revisionist historians resurrected them for reevaluation.

The second time Hoover resorted to an extensive moralistic analysis of American politics and economics occurred after the Great Depression had temporarily discredited his previous progressive and humanitarian record. After much reflection upon his role as titular head of the Republican party and increasing concern with the *methods* as well as the *substance* of New Deal programs, he published *Challenge to Liberty* in the fall of 1934. It did not receive the generally favorable bipartisan reception accorded *American Individualism* twelve years earlier; New Deal supporters immediately denounced this work as an anti-intellectual and unprogressive response to their urban brand of liberalism. From then until the present, the American public has regarded its dire predictions about New Deal measures leading to a fascistic American state as the last word on Hoover's reactionary political and economic thought.

Unfortunately, too many Hoover scholars, including myself, have tended to concentrate on the ideological consistency represented by these two theoretical works rather than noting the significantly different circumstances surrounding their appearance and his own political fortunes.[16] Following the publication of *American Individualism,* Hoover proceeded to implement certain programs as secretary of commerce and later president which he seldom justified exclusively, if at all, on the basis of the moral progressivism in this 1922 book. In contrast, he could neither subordinate nor exemplify through positive public action the ideas contained in *Challenge to Liberty* because, for the first time since 1900, Hoover occupied no major position of power within his profession or the government. Stripped of the power to act effectively on the national scene, all that was left of Hoover's progressivism was its rhetoric, which had always been more old-fashioned than his actions.[17]

Critics were quite right in pointing out that Hoover had never seemed so interested in employing liberty and freedom arguments before the New Deal. He had held such ideas but never felt obliged to justify his actions or programs principally upon them — not even during the presidential campaigns of 1928 and 1932. In *Challenge to Liberty,* however, he could not have sounded more like an old-time moral Progressive if he had tried, and now there were no actions to temper his rhetoric. Like so many other Progressives who finally refused to support the New Deal, Hoover used excessive language that made his arguments appear hysterical and unrelated to reality.[18] (I do not mean to imply by this that one cannot find basically sound criticisms of the New Deal if one delves beneath his rhetoric. Hoover raised enduring questions about what long term effects state capitalism would have on individual incentive, participatory democracy, and sense of community. He also was one of the first to note that New Deal measures did not end the depression.)

Logically, the idea of achieving efficiency through the elimination of wasteful production and organizational practices should have allowed him to link his anti-New Deal sentiment with his social engineering penchant for statistical analysis. The New Deal may not have been anywhere near as bad as Hoover prophesied, but one thing even New Dealers would not dispute was its inefficiency during and after the first Hundred Days. But by the fall of 1934, instead of countering the wasteful confusion of FDR's measures with facts and figures, Hoover had, for reasons that were not readily apparent, indiscriminately begun to equate the inefficiency of the New Deal with chaos, disintegration of individual freedom, violations of the Bill of Rights, and finally with Socialism and Fascism. He substituted arguments about preserving constitutional and spiritual values for factual analysis of FDR's policies. Thus within a year-and-one-half after leaving office, Hoover's public statements sounded like those of the classic Hofstadter Progressive, whose modern, twentieth-century reform ideas finally succumbed to an old-fashioned nineteenth-century upbringing.[19]

After examining Hoover's private 1933-35 correspondence with approximately twenty-five associates and friends, I can now document when and why he so quickly abandoned scientific progressivism for moralistic progressivism in responding to the New Deal. That he was bound to oppose the New Deal goes without saying, given the clearly defined limits he had always followed in trying to forge a voluntary, associational synthesis that would "reconcile a techno-corporate order with America's democratic heritage." While recent Hoover scholarship has clearly delineated the boundaries of his progressive philosophy, it has not adequately explained the sudden shift to an extreme moral rationalization of his highly complex "cooperative system."[20]

Ultimately, this switch in emphasis became a permanent one because Hoover had no opportunity to take concrete remedial action against the New Deal in his first years out of office. Consequently, he resorted to the one aspect of his long public life at which he was least adept: writing about theoretical abstractions. Previously, his progressive career and reputation had been based almost exclusively on compulsive activism. Now confined to writing about, rather than acting upon, his social control progressivism, it began to sound like a hell-fire and damnation fundamentalism.

Hoover's conversion on paper from engineer to evangelist was complete by the time he published *Challenge to Liberty*. The final triumph of his moralistic progressive instincts over his scientific ones can be attributed in large measure to the following events which occurred between his defeat at the polls in November, 1932, and September, 1934. First, he decided not to speak out publicly against the New Deal for the first eighteen months of its existence; second, his paranoia over smear tactics employed by the Democratic party before and during the presidential campaign, and what he perceived to be suppression of freedom of expression by the Roosevelt administration, increased as aspersions were cast on the activities of some of the former members of his administration; third, his closest economic advisers rejected a plan he devised in the fall of 1933 for returning the United States and eventually the world to a gold standard, leaving him without any concrete anti-New Deal alternative to propose to the public; and finally, he developed an obsessional preoccupation with proving that during the interregnum Roosevelt bore the primary responsibility for making the economic situation worse, in that the president-elect refused to state his monetary and fiscal intentions while conspiring behind the scenes to devalue the dollar and abandon the gold standard.[21]

Contrary to standard interpretations, therefore, Hoover's moral condemnation of the New Deal did not emerge full blown at the end of the 1932 presidential race, when he said in Madison Square Garden that the campaign was "a contest between two philosophies of government" rather than simply between two men or two political parties. It is true that within a few weeks of Roosevelt's inauguration Hoover wrote that his New York talk might "prove prophetic," and there is no doubt that such words as "socialism" and "fascism" appeared in his letters when he referred to the New Deal right after leaving office. In most of his correspondence, however, he insisted that in order "to stop this move to gigantic Socialism of America," Republicans had "to let the country know the real facts behind some of these things," such as the currency manipulation and planned economy ideas of the New Dealers. Likewise, in these letters in which Hoover referred to the hysterical actions of the Roosevelt administration, he almost always predicted that once the hysteria lessened the door would be open for a rational GOP counterattack.[22] Moreover, the bulk of his private correspondence during the spring and summer of 1933 is replete with detailed economic figures relating to legislation during the first Hundred Days and requests for more statistical data. In July, 1933, he talked of preparing factual articles on major New Deal monetary, agricultural, and industrial programs.[23]

What prevented these articles from materializing before the publication of *Challenge to Liberty* in September, 1934? In other words, why didn't Hoover publish the detailed economic information present in his correspondence in the spring and summer of 1933? The most obvious answer is that he was advised by all of his closest friends and political associates *not* to speak out against the Democrats. The first advice along these lines came before he left office. As early as February 2, 1933, John Callan O'Laughlin, editor of the *Army-Navy Journal*, warned that any immediate postpresidential statements by Hoover would be interpreted as an attempt at a political comeback, and that the best course of action would be to wait until the Republican party turned to him as the Democrats had turned to Cleveland in 1892.

Hoover repeatedly agreed with the advice of O'Laughlin and others, expressing his own conviction that it was not in the "national interest to engage in political activities . . . when the solidarity of national action is so desirable for the recovery of the nation." At the same time, however, he bitterly noted that the Democrats had not accorded him the same courtesy in the recent campaign. While he often expressed resentment about his agreed-upon silence, he usually concluded that "we must reserve our fire until we can make it effective."[24] Clearly, if his political friends did not want him to speak out, neither did his enemies within his own party, with whom he engaged in a struggle for control of the Republican National Committee in 1933 and 1934.[25]

This decision not to criticize New Deal policies in public was strongly reinforced by Hoover's growing conviction that the smear tactics employed against him by the Democratic National Committee during the 1932 election campaign had created a press environment uniformly hostile to his views. Indeed, the personal attack by the media and muckraking journalists on Hoover during the depression years would have left anyone slightly suspicious of receiving fair coverage. This suspicion influenced his decision not to speak out. He wrote in April, 1933: "I have your advice that I should not enter into the public discussion as they [the Democrats and the press] would use it only as a red-Herring and it would not save the day." In October, 1933, he complained more pessimistically to Christian Herter about the "total stifling of criticism," saying:

> The cry that even constructive suggestion is unpatriotic has been so generally adopted by the newspapers as to practically stamp out free speech. And yet the very continuance of democracy is wholly dependent upon unrestricted constructive criticism. Many times I have felt that I simply could not bear to keep still, but up to date I think it has been the right thing to do. There is some justification so far as I am concerned in the fact that many of these things in order to be driven out of the American blood must need fail of their own poison. If I were to attack them, then at the time of the inevitable failure the Republicans would be blamed with causing it and it would still leave the issue alive.[26]

Increasingly, therefore, during late 1933 and early 1934, Hoover's letters were filled with phrases like "continual and flagrant misrepresentation" and "new era of smearing." He often used words like "mud bath" or "mud guns" in describing attacks upon his supporters.[27]

These and similarly paranoid sounding perceptions convinced him that the Democrats were conducting an "industrious search for another Teapot Dome." In fact, this belief was not entirely unfounded. There is evidence that his mail had been tampered with on several occasions.[28] The Roosevelt administration brought charges of "collusion and fraud" against Hoover's postmaster general, Walter F. Brown, in connection with the awarding of air mail contracts. Income tax action had been taken against Secretary of the Treasury Andrew Mellon, and rumors of pending charges against Secretary of Agriculture Arthur Hyde and Attorney General William D. Mitchell abounded. Initially, even the early Nye committee hearings into the munitions industry appeared indirectly aimed at discrediting Hoover's effort on behalf of peace, in that they insinuated that he encouraged the manufacture and sale of war weapons. To top it all off, the New Dealers renamed Hoover Dam during their first months in office.[29]

Under such circumstances, Hoover began to view all actions taken by the Democrats against his administration or him personally, as well as those taken to fight the depression, as attempts "to stamp out free speech and free debate in the United States." He believed that certain economic interests (largely those which dominated the drafting of the NRA codes) were allied with New Dealers in censoring his use of the press and radio because "the business world everywhere is complaining . . . against any criticism, constructive or otherwise, as 'it discourages recovery.' " All of this led him not only to the conclusion that the "public does not wish to hear from me — yet at least," but also that there was a national conspiracy to silence him. Thus the ex-president began to question all New Deal methods, regardless of the specific substance of the program involved, as undemocratic and potentially dangerous to freedom of speech and other constitutional rights.[30] By the time Hoover reached this stage and decided he must speak out to warn people against the long range threats posed by the statist corporatism of the Roosevelt administration, he no longer thought that hard, cold facts could turn the tide against the effect of collectivism on traditional American institutions, particularly individual rights.

"To me the Bill of Rights is the heart of the Constitution," he wrote to his friend, diplomat William R. Castle, Jr., on November 15, 1933. "All the rest is a method and a framework for its guardianship and development." Hoover repeatedly referred to the Bill of Rights in his private letters, saying that it created "an ordered individual liberty" and expressing the fear that the "whole temper and attitude of the Democratic Party is to break down this system and to substitute a regimentation of men and collectivism instead of a nation of freemen." Writing to Ashmun Brown in March, 1934, he claimed that the New Deal was transforming the government — from one where the individual has certain rights which could not be transgressed, even by the state, into one "where the individual is solely the pawn of the state. It is a lot worse than communism." Later in 1934, as he continued to watch the New Deal take form, he was more explicit about the effect of collectivism on American institutions. He argued in *Challenge to Liberty* that the "penetration of Socialist methods even to a partial degree will demoralize the economic system, the legislative bodies, and in fact the whole system of ordered Liberty." He went on to predict that the reaction to such demoralization "will not be more Socialism but will be toward Fascism because it has been the invariable turn in foreign countries where there is a considerable economic middle class. And this group is proportionately larger in the United States than in any other country in the world."[31]

What all of this meant is that Hoover had remained silent too long. With the publication of *Challenge to Liberty*, he had abandoned his belief in the efficacy of factual opposition to the New Deal and never published the statistical information he had on the NRA or AAA. However, it should be noted that these issues always took a back seat to the monetary and fiscal matters with which Hoover had been so concerned during the last months of his administration.

There is another reason for his failure to present hard data to the American public on specific New Deal measures. From the moment he left office he had collected material primarily on two interrelated subjects: the devaluation of the American dollar and the abandonment of the gold standard. He tried to use this information to prove that there had been collusion among FDR, certain members of the Federal Reserve Board, and leading eastern financiers on the question of devaluation *during* the interregnum, and to show that it was possible to return to the gold standard. He presented his findings on the gold question first. After working the entire summer of 1933 on "an idea for the restoration of gold currency and breaking down the artificial international famine in gold," Hoover submitted the idea to several trusted financial advisers, such as E. W. Kemmerer, Professor of Economics at Princeton; Lewis L. Strauss; and Adolph Miller. All of the replies now available in his postpresidential papers rejected the plan as unworkable.[32]

It is difficult to ascertain the exact impact these negative opinions had on Hoover, but one thing is clear. He had fought harder on the question of maintaining a gold standard, which was central to all of his economic foreign policy plans, than on any other issue (outside of the banking crisis) before leaving office. Now he had to face the fact that his plan for restoring confidence in American currency at home and abroad was not possible along the lines he had proposed. Moreover, the new gold policy of the Democrats, establishing the "commodity dollar," went into effect on October 25, 1933, forcing him to reevaluate his original calculations about the impact of further depreciation of the dollar in relation to world prices.

Caught slightly off balance by what he called "this latest experiment," he admitted he would have to defer presenting his own plan until he could judge the effect of the administration's. As a result, it was not until 1935 that he actually issued a comprehensive public statement on returning to the gold standard. And by then it was much too late to influence public policy. Even Hoover had to admit there was little likelihood of restoring the country's currency to gold: "I should of course like a vindication of my assurance that we could not go off the gold standard without chaos, but at the moment I fear going on to old values may be a double dose of chaos."[33]

While Hoover was first devising ideas for returning to the gold standard in the summer of 1933, he also had two of his former secretaries and a few other close associates carrying on a private investigation to determine when Roosevelt had decided to devalue the dollar. He finally concluded it had taken place at a meeting in Hyde Park on December 17 or 18, 1932. The correspondence on this issue is both extensive and confusing, but from it Hoover concluded the following: (1) there had been a conspiracy on the part of the incoming administration to undermine the credit and confidence of the nation, thereby unnecessarily precipitating the March, 1933, banking crisis; (2) subsequent depreciation of the dollar had not caused a significant rise in international commodity prices, as promised by Roosevelt, and that in fact "the effect of our going off the gold standard and our depreciation of the dollar" actually contributed to a lowering of world prices.[34]

The combination of the rejection of his gold standard plan with what he believed to be a conspiracy by the Roosevelt administration regarding monetary and fiscal policies — which it attempted to cover up with "fabricated statistics" — led Hoover to equate liberty and other constitutional rights with the gold standard. This was not as great a leap as it appears, given the circumstances just described, but his language makes it sound as though it were:

The very safety of liberty, as well as the right to property honestly won, rests upon sound convertible gold currency, and honest performance by the Government of its covenanted obligations, honest presentation of government expenditures, and a maintenance of government credit. There was no justification for the abandonment of the gold standard, and the paralysis that it has brought to long term credit and consequently to the capital goods industries with extended employment, is evident on every hand. . . . The creation of an extraordinary budget, the setting up of the Secretary of Agriculture with the power of independent taxation upon the food of the nation, and its expenditure without Congressional appropriation, the diversion of the RFC from its purpose of loans on sound security which were no burden on the taxpayer to the expenditure of unrecoverable money, are all of them methods of obscuring the riot of spending now in progress in Washington. Prosperity cannot be restored by the destruction of wealth or by the squandering of public money. . . . The framing of the Constitution and the protection of the Bill of Rights were designed to create an ordered individual liberty upon which this country has advanced beyond all nations of the world. It has never been a conception of the American people that individual liberty should transgress the common welfare. Laissez-faire has never been the basis of our social organization. Social justice and a just distribution of the fruits of industry and toil have ever been its first consideration. The American system of individualism differs from all other systems in its ideal that there should be an equal opportunity to all. The whole temper and attitude of the Democratic Party is to break down this system and to substitute a regimentation of men and collectivism instead of a nation of free men. Bureaucracy has already reached astounding dimensions, and the daily fear and terrorization imposed by them has been poured into every town and village.[35]

There is one last moral twist to Hoover's critique of the New Deal. I mentioned it earlier in connection with his lifelong battle against inefficiency and waste as an engineer, as director of food relief, and as secretary of commerce. From the beginning Hoover and his friends had not thought Roosevelt competent for the presidency. At best, they viewed FDR as a political opportunist; at worst, as confused and "amateurish." In any case, they believed that the Roosevelt administration, with its inept personnel, produced chaos, waste, and inefficiency.[36] It was an endless cycle that could not be broken by statistical refutation, especially given alleged media bias. It could only be effectively attacked on high sounding moral and constitutional grounds. Or so Hoover thought. Perhaps he had always believed that waste and inefficiency and chaos were immoral. But at earlier stages in his career he had combated them more with action than with words. Now he was reduced to tilting at New

Deal windmills with rhetoric alone — truly the Don Quixote of the old-time Progressives.

Sometime in the summer of 1934, while writing *Challenge to Liberty*, Hoover decided that however disturbing the substance of specific New Deal programs was, New Deal methods had to be countered first and foremost because they constituted the long term threat to the American system as Hoover perceived it. NRAs and AAAs would come and go; it was the general method of saving capitalism through massive state intervention that Hoover refused to accept.[37] He wanted to save the American people from the New Deal whether they wanted to be saved or not. In this case they didn't, and so he couldn't. Even if Hoover had spoken out unequivocally in the spring and summer of 1933 with the facts and figures at his command on the NRA codes and AAA measures, it is still doubtful that he could have convinced the public to abandon the New Deal. But he might have been able to salvage some remnants of his scientific progressivism and his earlier reform reputation in the eyes of his contemporaries.

This explanation is not meant to justify Hoover's ideological limitations. Rather, it is an attempt to explain why he and other perfectly reasonable Progressives could have viewed New Deal fiscal and monetary methods as essentially unconstitutional and therefore a threat to liberty that could only be opposed in morally righteous terms. With the exception of a handful of radical agrarians, many former Progressives logically refused to accept the "liberalism" of the Roosevelt administration.[38] Their choice of language delayed and in some instances temporarily discredited serious study of their views. Their response, however, was no less progressive for being expressed in traditional terms. In retrospect, these Progressives were correct in perceiving the significant structural and attitudinal difference between the New Era and the New Deal — a difference that possibly seems more important for the 1970s than it did for the 1930s.

NOTES

1   Articles published in *Agricultural History*, 51 (April 1977), by Martin L. Fausold, Gary H. Koerselman, and Joan Hoff Wilson place Hoover's agricultural policies in the broader context of his views on corporatism and international trade. When I began to investigate Hoover's early postpresidential correspondence for this paper, I anticipated finding more material on agricultural matters in order to see how they compared with Haugen's and Wallace's. This did not prove possible because the bulk of his correspondence through the summer and fall of 1933 concentrated on monetary and fiscal matters. Characteristically, agricultural issues figured only peripherally in his mind as they related to the general economic picture.

2   *New York Times*, Jan. 12, 1979, C19; *New York Times Book Review*, Feb. 4, 1979, 11; *Chronicle of Higher Education*, Feb. 20, 1979, 8-9; *New Republic*, March 10, 1979, 35-36; Arthur M. Schlesinger, Jr., "Hoover Makes a Comeback," *New York Review of Books*, March 8, 1979, 10-16.

3   This description of progressivism is drawn generally from the theories of Robert H. Wiebe and Otis L. Graham, Jr., although my first views of the contradictory or paradoxical aspects of the movement and many of those participating in it came from the ideas of Herbert Croly and Richard Hofstadter. If Progressives like Hoover, who rejected the New Deal, are to be accorded status as legitimate reformers, the differences in attitudes and methods between the Progressive movement and the New Deal must be distinguished from what appears to be the same goal: rationalization of a corporatist economic system.

4   Otis L. Graham, Jr., *The Great Campaigns: Reform and War in America, 1900-1928* (Englewood Cliffs, N.J., 1971), 128-29.

5   Edwin T. Layton, Jr., *The Revolt of the Engineers: Social Responsibility of the American Engineering Profession* (Cleveland, 1971), 134-200; Jean Christie, "Morris Llewellyn Cooke: Progressive Engineer" (Ph.D. dissertation, Columbia University, 1963); David Burner, *Herbert Hoover: A Public Life* (New York, 1979), 63-71.

6   Joan Hoff Wilson, *Herbert Hoover: Forgotten Progressive* (Boston, 1975), 39-40.

7   Layton, 53-74, 142-43, 148, 193, 235.

8   James S. Olson, "The Philosophy of Herbert Hoover: A Contemporary Perspective," *Annals of Iowa*, 43 (winter 1976), 181-91; Wilson, *Hoover*, 41-64.

9   Schlesinger, "Hoover Makes a Comeback," 14, 16.

10   House Diary, Feb. 25, 1920. Quoted from copy at the Herbert Hoover Presidential Library (hereafter cited as HHPL); E. Daniel Potts, "The Progressive Profile in Iowa," *Mid-America*, 47 (April 1965), 257-68. Hoover's old friend, former secretary of the interior Ray Lyman Wilbur, tried unsuccessfully to convince Charles and Mary Beard that they should incorporate a progressive reinterpretation of Hoover in their *Basic History of the United States*, making the following comparison with Theodore Roosevelt:

> I would not suggest that Mr. Hoover was the originator of liberalism or of the ideas of progressive reforms — neither was Theodore Roosevelt. My statement was merely that Hoover was a greater force in bringing the Republican Party to a progressive point of view than was Theodore Roosevelt. As you say, Roosevelt split his Party and the ultra-conservatives regained control of it after the war — as expressed in Harding and Coolidge. Hoover did reverse them, and went further in philosophy and action than Theodore Roosevelt ever proposed, and they have so retained. No doubt the ideas of both were imbibed from other persons.
>   I do not believe anyone can read the writings of both Theodore Roosevelt and Hoover without realizing that there is a far greater depth of thought in Hoover, and that thought, expressed now over twenty-five years, had had much more effect on public thinking than Theodore Roosevelt's.

Needless to say, the Beards ignored this attempt to influence their textbook image of Hoover. See Wilbur to Charles A. Beard, Aug. 30, Oct. 9, 1944, Charles A. Beard, Correspondence and Supplementary Material, in Herbert Hoover Post-Presidential Papers, Individual File, HHPL; Beard to Hoover, Sept. 20, 1944 (quoted in letter from Miriam Vagts, March 30, 1971). Hereafter, all correspondence cited may be found in the Herbert Hoover Post-Presidential Papers, Individual File, HHPL, except where otherwise noted.

11   Hoover to Taft, June 17, 1920, Robert A. Taft Papers, Box 1179, Library of Congress.

12   Since 1919 Hoover had argued in favor of graduated inheritance taxes and for heavier taxation of upper incomes in order to insure a fairer distribution of wealth. See Herbert Hoover Public Statements, nos. 39 (Dec. 29, 1919) and 2318 (Sept. 30, 1936), HHPL. Also see Burner,

146-47. Sullivan felt so strongly about what he thought were excessive Republican bond issues for road building that he wrote to Josephus Daniels on December 8, 1922, complaining about the "new progressive movement in the Republican party" that Hoover was heading: "I am decidedly disturbed by a conception of progressivism which includes high taxation and prodigal expenditures with the public money .... It is because [of] ... this conception of the public revenues that I hesitate to go along with them [the new Republican Progressive leaders like Hoover] as wholeheartedly as I did with the old insurgent and progressive movement in 1912." Mark Sullivan Papers, Hoover Institution on War, Revolution and Peace, Stanford, California.

13   Wilson, *Hoover*, 74-75, 123-24; Ronald L. Feinman, "The Progressive Republican Senate Bloc and the Presidential Election of 1912," *Mid-America*, 59 (April-July 1977), 73-82; Philip A. Grant, "The Presidential Election of 1932 in Iowa," *Annals of Iowa*, 44 (winter 1979), 541-50; Graham, *Great Campaigns*, 114-17; *idem, An Encore for Reform: The Old Progressives and the New Deal* (New York, 1967), 24-43.

14   Hoover to Verne Marshall, May 16, 1933. Also see Hoover to Arthur M. Hyde, Jan. 27, 1934; Hoover to Frank B. Knox, Aug. 30, 1934; Hoover to Harvey Ingham, Sept. 7, 1934; Theodore Joslin to Hoover, Dec. 8, 1934; Joslin to Hoover, undated (1934), March 8, Aug. 5, 1935; Hyde to Hoover, Nov. 28, 1933; Hoover to Ogden Mills, Nov. 18, 1933; Hoover to Knox, Nov. 28, 1933, Feb. 19, 1934; Patrick Hurley to Hoover, May 26, Aug. 25, 1933; Carl Hanna to Hoover, Feb. 22, 1935; and, in O'Laughlin Papers, Boxes 43-44, Library of Congress: John Callan O'Laughlin to Hoover, March 25, 1933; Hoover to O'Laughlin, March 29, 1933, Jan. 6, March 5, 1934, and undated (1934).

15   Criticism of the Liberty League abounds in the Hoover postpresidential papers. For a representative sample see: Hoover to Ashmun Brown, Sept. 5, 1934; Hurley to Hoover, Sept. 5, 6, 1934; and undated 1934 letter to O'Laughlin cited in fn. 14. For other critics of the New Deal and members of the Old Right, see: Leonard P. Liggio, "A New Look at Robert A. Taft," paper delivered at the 1973 American Historical Association convention; John Braeman, *et al.*, eds., *The New Deal: The National Level* (Columbus, O., 1975), 26-33; James T. Patterson, *Congressional Criticism and the New Deal* (Lexington, Ky., 1967); George Wolfskill, *The Revolt of the Conservatives: A History of the American Liberty League, 1934-1940* (Boston, 1962); Ronald Radosh, *Prophets on the Right: Profiles of Conservative Critics of American Globalism* (New York, 1975); and Graham, *Encore for Reform*, 195-204.

16   This is true of all recent studies of Hoover, whether they praise or criticize him. See Olson, "Philosophy of Hoover;" Wilson, *Hoover*; Burner, *Hoover*; Elliot A. Rosen, *Hoover, Roosevelt and the Brains Trust* (New York, 1977); Gary Dean Best, *The Politics of American Individualism* (Westport, Conn., 1975).

17   Howard W. Runkel, "Hoover's Speeches During His Presidency" (Ph.D. dissertation, Stanford University, 1950). Hoover's talks were dull, repetitious, and filled with statistics. See Wilson, *Hoover*, 127-28; Burner, 314-15. Contrary to the impression created in Rosen's book, he did not constantly refer in the 1920s to the general themes he raised in *American Individualism*.

18   Richard Hofstadter, *The Age of Reform* (New York, 1966), 300-26; Graham, *Encore for Reform, 24-100; Frank Annunziata,* "The Progressive as Conservative: George Creel's Quarrel with New Deal Liberalism," *Wisconsin Magazine of History*, 57 (spring 1974), 220-33. I am referring to the language and tone of his *The Challenge to Liberty* (New York, 1934) and most of his other published speeches on the New Deal, which can be found in Hoover's *Addresses Upon the American Road, 1933-1938* (New York, 1938), *American Ideals versus the New Deal* (New York, 1936), and *America's Way Forward* (New York, 1939).

19   Hoover to John Richardson, May 9, 1933; Hoover to Ashmun Brown, Nov. 16, 1933; Hoover to Hyde, Jan. 27, 29, 1934; Hoover to William D. Mitchell, Sept. 18, 1934; Hoover to Alf Landon, Feb. 26, 1935; Hoover to O'Laughlin, Oct. 12, 1933 (O'Laughlin Papers, Box 43). These are simply samples of many such statements. They increase markedly toward the end of 1933 and the beginning of 1934.

20   The essays of Ellis W. Hawley represent the best explanation of the characteristics of Hoover's brand of corporatism. See in particular his essays in Martin Fausold, ed., *The Hoover Presidency: A Reappraisal* (Albany, 1974), 101-22; Braeman, *et al.*, 50-82; and J. Joseph Huthmacher and Warren I. Susman, eds., *Herbert Hoover and the Crisis of American Capitalism* (Cambridge, Mass., 1973), 1-33.

21   Susan Estabrook Kennedy, *The Banking Crisis of 1933* (Lexington, Ky., 1973), 68-69, 135-38, points out how illogical this last preoccupation was, but it must be remembered that it fit in with other conspiracy theories Hoover held concerning New Deal policies and thus played a crucial role in his shift to moral progressivism.

22   Hoover to O'Laughlin, March 25, 29, Oct. 12, 1933 (O'Laughlin Papers, Box 43); Hoover to Hyde, March 31, 1933, Jan. 30, 1934; Hoover to Bruce Barton, Oct. 3, 1933; Hoover to Mills, May 7, 1933; Hoover to Knox, March 25, 1933, March 10, 1935.

23   Hoover's correspondence with Lewis L. Strauss, Walter F. Brown, Arch W. Shaw, Adolph Miller, E.W. Kemmerer, Mills, and Richardson is the best source for this exchange of factual information, especially about monetary and fiscal matters. For his intention to write factual articles, see Hoover to Mills, July 26, 1933.

24   O'Laughlin to Hoover, Feb. 2, 1933; Hoover to O'Laughlin, Feb. 3, April 28, Aug. 22, 1933 — all in O'Laughlin Papers, Box 43; Hoover to Hyde, March 31, 1933; Hoover to Strauss (telegram), June 25, 1933; Hoover to Winfield Jones, Aug. 14, 1933; Hoover to Richardson, May 9, 1933; and, in Castle Papers, HHPL, Hoover to William R. Castle, Jr., March 10, 1934.

25   Wilson, *Hoover*, 216-33. Generally speaking, his correspondence with Ashmun Brown, O'Laughlin, Joslin, Hurley, Knox, Hyde, Castle, and Landon represents the best source for political struggles within the GOP.

26   Hoover to O'Laughlin, April 28, 1933 (O'Laughlin Papers, Box 43); Hoover to Christian Herter, Oct. 4, 1933.

27   Hoover to O'Laughlin, July 4, Dec. 7, 1933 (O'Laughlin Papers, Box 43); Hoover to Richardson, Feb. 19, 1934; Hoover to Roy Howard, Feb. 27, 1934; Hoover to Ashmun Brown, March 13, 1934; Hoover to Knox, March 10, April 20, Aug. 20, 1934; Hoover to Hurley, Sept. 11, 1934; Hoover to Strauss, Sept. 21, Oct. 1, 1934; Hoover to Hugh Gibson, Aug. 23, 1934; Hoover to Hyde, Oct. 1, 1934; Hoover to Joslin, Dec. 13, 1934.

28   Hoover to Castle, May 8, 1934 (Castle Papers); Hoover to Walter F. Brown, March 7, 1934, and Brown to Hoover, March 12, 1934. Most of the evidence of mail tampering was in connection with the investigation of the air mail contracts. Quote is from Hoover to Ashmun Brown, March 13, 1934.

29   Over 200 pages of material on the controversy over air mail contracts, some of which were summarily cancelled by Roosevelt's postmaster general, James Farley, can be found in the Hoover Post-Presidential Papers, Subject File, Air Mail Controversy. Hoover to Ashmun Brown, March 13, 1934; Hoover to Joslin, Dec. 15, 1934; Hurley to Hoover, Dec. 6, 1934; Hoover to Walter F. Brown, May 3, 1934; Hoover to Harry Chandler, April 20, 1934; Herbert Hoover, *Memoirs* (New York, 1952), III, 453-57.

30   Hoover to Castle, Jan. 16, 1934 (Castle Papers); Hoover to Hyde, Jan. 27, 29, 30, 1934; Hoover to Richardson, Feb. 19, 1934; Hoover to Landon, Feb. 26, 1935; Hoover to William Allen White, May 10, 1935; Hoover to Ashmun Brown, Nov. 16, 1933. Hoover's fears were reinforced by many of his correspondents. See Edmond Lincoln to Hoover, Jan. 5, 1934; Ingham to Hoover, Oct. 1, 1934, June 18, 1935; Hyde to Hoover, Sept. 13, Dec. 3, 1934.

31   Hoover to Castle, Nov. 15, 1933 (Castle Papers); Hoover to Ashmun Brown, March 13, 1934; Hoover, *Challenge*, 60-61.

32   Hoover's plan proposed that the U.S. and Britain agree to "institute a buyer's strike in gold," which he thought would reduce its price to old parities because it would increase the amount available for purchase. For two detailed responses concerning its weaknesses, see Strauss to Hoover, Sept. 14, 1933, and Kemmerer to Hoover, Oct. 19, 1933. For other comments on gold, see Hoover to Shaw, Feb. 17, 1933; Hoover to Mills, June 13, 1933; Hoover to Kemmerer, Oct. 12, 1933; Hoover to Walter F. Brown, Oct. 22, 1933; Hoover to Mills, Nov. 15, 1933; Hoover to O'Laughlin, Dec. 5, 1933.

33   Hoover to O'Laughlin, Oct. 24, Nov. 13, Dec. 5, 1933; Hoover to Walter Lichtenstein, Jan. 12, 1935. His immediate response to the "commodity dollar" was to begin to point out in November to a number of his correspondents that "depreciation of the dollar by 17 per cent since October 22 has increased commodity prices by less than 2 per cent. The 2 per cent is of course due to international commodities which is natural, but Old Man Supply and Demand seems to be still dominant in the field of domestic commodities and it will take some time for him to appreciate the effect of a depreciated dollar..." Hoover to Shaw, Nov. 16, 1933; Hoover to Richardson, Nov. 14, 1933; Hoover to Lincoln, Nov. 13, 1933. When he did finally speak out in 1935, his remarks were in part motivated by the Supreme Court decision in the Government Bond cases (ruling that the bonds could not be redeemed in gold despite clauses to that effect in them). His friends generally agreed with his condemnation of the decision as one more example of a "gross violation of the Constitution by men who had taken an oath to sustain it, and because they can get away with the violation, there is to be no moral indignation." Hoover to Hyde, Feb. 25, 1935.

34   Most of his correspondence with one of his former private secretaries, Lawrence Richey, on this subject can be found in Adolph Miller's Individual File, instead of under Richey's name. Much of the rest of it is in correspondence with Joslin and some with Ashmun Brown. For a standard summary of what he thought to be conclusive proof of a conspiracy, see Hoover to Ashmun Brown (Nov. 1934); Hoover to Joslin, Dec. 7, 1934; Hoover to Kemmerer, May 19, 1933; Hoover to Lincoln, Dec. 5, 1933; Hoover to A.C. Mattei, Dec. 27, 1933; Hyde to Hoover, Feb. 20, 1935 (confirming Hoover's conspiracy thesis); Marshall to Hoover, March 13, 1935; Hoover to Marshall, March 16, 1935; Hoover to Ingham, June 21, 1935; Hoover to James Rand (under Knox, Individual File), Feb. 25, 1933.

35   Hoover to O'Laughlin, Oct. 12, 1933, Aug. 31, 1934 (O'Laughlin Papers, Boxes 43-44). See also Hoover to Hyde, Jan. 27, 29, 1934.

36   Hoover to Knox, March 25, 1933, March 22, 1935; Hoover to Rand (under Knox, Individual File), Feb. 25, 1933; Hoover to Mills, June 23, 1933; Strauss to Hoover, May 4, 1934; Paul Wooton to Hoover, March 20, 1933; Richardson to Hoover, May 2, June 28, 1933; Hoover to Joslin, July 3, 1933, May 30, 1934.

37   His comments on the NRA and AAA are disappointing because they are not nearly as detailed as his comments on monetary and fiscal policy. For samples see Hoover to O'Laughlin, April 28, 1933 (O'Laughlin Papers, Box 43); Hoover to O'Laughlin, April 19, 28, Aug. 9, 1933; Hoover to Joslin, May 19, 1933 (claiming credit for FDR's refinancing of farm and home mortgage legislation), Hoover to Mitchell, Dec. 27, 1933; Hoover to Knox, July 9, 1934; Hoover

to Ashmun Brown, Aug. 23, 1934; Hyde to Hoover, Dec. 19, 1935 (claiming the New Deal took over certain aspects of the original Hoover farm program in the wake of the Supreme Court decision striking down the first AAA); Hoover to Hyde, March 25, 1933, Dec. 22, 1935; Hoover to Joslin, Aug. 2, 1933; Hoover to Hurley, Jan. 4, 1934; Strauss to Hoover, March 9, 1934; Hoover to Knox, Aug. 23, 1934.

38 For difficulties even some of the agrarian supporters of the New Deal had with the AAA, see articles by Richard Lowitt, James L. Forsythe, and Irvin May, Jr., in *Agricultural History*, 51 (April 1977); Graham, *Encore for Reform*, 94-100, *passim*.

Henry A. Wallace in 1929

HENRY AGARD WALLACE
AND THE PROGRESSIVE FAITH

THEODORE A. WILSON

TO BE HONEST, the task which I assumed some months ago by accepting the very kind invitation to participate in this symposium—to identify the "progressive" elements in the thoughts and actions of Henry Agard Wallace and to suggest appropriate insights that the study of Wallace's career can contribute to our understanding of the larger patterns in progressive thought and the history of the Progressive movement—has proved exceedingly difficult. I have had, in fact, the experience of suffering "writer's block" in the effort to fulfill this assignment. Indeed, Professor Lowitt and you, the audience, may not permit me any claim of fulfillment once you have listened to what follows.

The principal reason for the difficult time I have experienced with this paper is that, though I have been living with Henry Agard Wallace for, now, almost ten years, I have rarely thought of him as a "Progressive"—that is, *big P* Progressive. The connections are all there, of course (the family tradition of support for and participation in progressive politics, Henry A. Wallace's early and intense involvement with progressive issues and personalities, his immersion in McNary-Haugenism, the use of *Wallaces' Farmer* as a pulpit from which to advocate progressive dogma); but the relative youth and lack of political visibility of Henry A. Wallace during the sunset decade of progressive politics, the 1920s, have tended to obscure the abiding influence of progressivism on Wallace's views and on his political career. As time passed, Henry A. Wallace may have abandoned the youthful and enthusiastic commitment to such progressive shibboleths as rigorous enforcement of the antitrust laws, the battle against monopoly, and efficiency in government. He succeeded in gaining control over powerful feelings of revulsion against cities, those "Babylons . . . cancerous growths" blighting the good land, and to some degree, therefore, he accommodated a deeply ingrained agrarianism to the reality of an urban America.[1] However, Wallace never abandoned what to some historians is the core of progressive ideology, the belief in politics as a forum for moral questions and a concomitant commitment to social justice and the abundant life for all. In his "Reminiscences," the five thousand-plus page

Theodore A. Wilson is Professor of History, University of Kansas.

transcription of interviews conducted by the Columbia Oral History Collection, Wallace recalled that as a very young man he became obsessed with the question of what was "worthwhile" in life, with "what is the chief end of man." His lifelong search for the answer to that question was to take him down some surprising pathways. But Wallace never lost faith—a "progressive" faith—that there was an ultimate meaning to life, one capable of political definition, and that moral energy could make it reality. "I've always believed that if you envision something that hasn't been, that can be, and bring it into being, that it is a tremendously worthwhile thing to do," Wallace observed many years later.[2] Whether this be an expression of "mysticism," "optimism," or "progressivism" perhaps is not as significant as the fact that Wallace espoused an activist creed and applied it to the improvement of corn, strawberries, agricultural prices relative to industrial earnings, and society in general.

Gilbert Fite and Joan Hoff Wilson have presented for your consideration two Iowans whose careers may be taken as exemplifying rather widely disparate elements in that complex, amorphous body of historical phenomena termed progressivism. The third Iowan with whom we are dealing today, Henry A. Wallace, shared many of their concerns. There are other connections as well. Even though somewhat younger than either Haugen or Hoover, he served for several years as a close political ally of the former and for several decades as a bitter personal and political enemy of the latter. Of course, Wallace went on to participate in the establishment of the New Deal, that system of state-managed capitalism and broker politics which supplanted the "old Progressive dream of an agrarian commonwealth."[3] In accommodating so easily to the enormous expansion of the state and its power over people, Wallace proved more pragmatic than either Haugen or Hoover. He was concerned, however, much less with ideological purity or consistency than with the reformation of human nature. Commenting with rare insight, John Blum has observed of Henry A. Wallace: "He was an austere moralist, impatient less with impiety than with sloth, deceit, selfishness, and materialism."[4] One may even assert that Wallace was as eager as Walter Rauschenbusch or Washington Gladden to usher in the "Kingdom of God on earth," although his notion of what constituted this glorious and sacred commonwealth (and what was necessary to bring it into being) differed markedly from the vision of more conventionally religious reformers. The emphasis here is on the 1920s, even though the New Deal was to see the zenith of Wallace's efforts on behalf of liberal (some would say progressive) economic and social programs, and in 1948 he would be the standard bearer of a reincarnated Progressive party. However, those activities belonged to a wholly different ideological and political context and are not, therefore, considered here.

1

Three influences predominated in the development of Henry A. Wallace's political and social views: family, location, and religion. Of course, in fact Henry A. Wallace did not—could not—separate these influences, for they represented within his personal experience three equal and identical sides of a triangle. To a Wallace, family meant Iowa meant agriculture meant Protestant activism.

Henry Agard Wallace was the scion of a family which had attained a position of considerable eminence in Iowa during the Progressive era. (Notably, the Wallaces considered Herbert Hoover a political upstart simply because they had never heard of him before the name of "the wonder worker from Iowa" began to appear in the newspapers.⁵) Henry A.'s grandfather, "Uncle Henry," in some ways the most remarkable of all the Wallaces, studied for a career in the ministry, volunteered as a chaplain in the Union Army, and served Presbyterian churches in Illinois and eastern Iowa. Forced by ill health (and the erosion of his sense of calling) to leave the ministry, Henry Wallace took up farming and settled in Winterset, Iowa, in 1877. He became a pillar of the community, the Presbyterian church, and, as well, the Republican party. The latter allegiance was conditional, for "both major political parties continually disappointed the Wallaces," as one biographer has noted.⁶ In the 1890s "Uncle Henry" began to publish an agricultural newspaper, *Wallaces' Farmer,* in Des Moines. His son, Henry C., having been both a farmer and a college professor, moved his family (which included Henry A., the eldest child, born in 1888) from Ames to Des Moines and joined the new farm journal.

During the next decade "Uncle Henry" and Henry C. obtained from *Wallaces' Farmer* a sizable fortune and an even more substantial reputation for leadership in agricultural and political circles. In the context of the times, the Wallaces were forward-looking, even "progressive." They were supporters of reform though emphatically not of "radical" solutions to current problems.⁷

Henry A. Wallace was greatly influenced by his grandfather. He was especially taken with "Uncle Henry's" powerful rhetoric, couched always in biblical phraseology, inveighing against the evil trusts—"the most complete and effective instrument[s] for robbery yet devised"—and heralding the dawn of a Christian cooperative commonwealth.⁸ His grandfather's experiences as a leading member of the Country Life Commission appointed by President Theodore Roosevelt, as a powerful figure among agrarian Republicans ("Uncle Henry" several times was offered the post of secretary of agriculture), and as an energetic supporter of Bull Moose progressivism in 1912 deeply affected Henry A. Wallace.

Less obvious but still very strong was the influence of Henry C. Wallace. Although his father appeared to be decidedly more conservative and "practical" than his unpredictable, stargazing son, Henry A. Wallace believed that the differences between them—"Harry's" fondness for golf, country clubs, and cocktails, compared with Henry A.'s fascination with testing hybrids, corn shows, and soya extract—were superficial. That extended to the decision of Henry C. Wallace to accept appointment as secretary of agriculture in the administration of Warren G. Harding, a step that might have opened a gulf but did not. "As a matter of fact," Henry A. Wallace argued later, "Father's attitude on many things was identical with my own. He happened to be in a Republican cabinet, and I was later on in a Democratic cabinet. But there was very little difference between our attitudes."[9] In these formative years Henry A. Wallace was introduced (partly through family discussions) to major figures in progressive thought: Herbert Croly, John Dewey, Charles Beard, Richard T. Ely, and others. He was attracted in particular by the provocative if murky arguments of Thorstein Veblen, whose harsh assessment of modern society, *Theory of the Leisure Class*, he first read in 1916. From Veblen, Henry A. Wallace adapted the concept of "cultural lag," of the failure of social, economic, and political institutions to keep up with the progress of science and technology. Much like Herbert Hoover, he prophesied the emergence of "a technologically dynamic society dedicated to the efficient making and sharing of industrial and agricultural commodities, a society that would need scientists and managers to fashion an abundant life for the common man."[10] He presented an explicit statement of this positivist faith in *Wallaces' Farmer* in February, 1923:

> When we see the world being molded from the world as it is to the world as we want it, nobody invents utopias.
>
> They aren't needed.
>
> We know that the ideal state is on the way.
>
> It is when things look dark, when nihilism impends, when life seems meaningless and futile, that we become aware of the gap between life as we live it and life as we want it.
>
> Then life as we want it becomes embodied in some ideal plan, some utopia that we create in the air because we are sadly conscious that we have lost it on earth.
>
> This is a period particularly favorable to the development of utopias.
>
> Everyone, whether he be conservative or liberal, objects to the world as he finds it at this minute.
>
> Our conservatives look to find their utopias in the return to the happy past that probably never existed.
>
> Our liberals expect to find their utopias in a no doubt impossibly happy future that is to be here tomorrow.
>
> This habit of creating utopias gets a good deal of ridicule that it does not deserve.
>
> The utopia that is devised not as a means of escape from life, but as

a means of reconstructing it, is a vital factor in the development of civilization.

We need, especially when the times are out of joint, to have men consider what the good life is and how to get it.

Our utopias are the blueprints of our future civilization, and as such, airy structures though they are, they really play a bigger part in the progress of man than our more material structures of brick and steel.

The habit of building utopias shows to a degree whether a race is made up of dull-spirited bipeds or whether it is made up of men who want to enjoy the full savoring of existence that only comes when they feel themselves working with the forces of nature to remake a world nearer to their heart's desire.[11]

The thrust of these sentiments is, of course, faith that the creation of Henry A. Wallace's "utopia"—the progressive commonwealth—was inevitable. As more information about the "good" was obtained, people, as rational beings, would use this data to change and perfect the physical and social environment. Although the nature of his utopia changed over the next forty years, Henry A. Wallace never lost faith in its inevitability or the essential rationality of humankind.[12]

2

When his father left Des Moines for Washington in 1921, Henry A. Wallace assumed total editorial responsibility for *Wallaces' Farmer*. The demands of this position—keeping abreast of technological, financial, and political developments of concern to Iowa and midwestern farmers, interpreting national and international issues to readers and advertisers, representing "Iowa" before regional and national organizations—reinforced Henry A.'s strong ties to the land, to Iowa, and to rural life. As was noted earlier, he was committed to the primacy of agrarian "civilization" and of rural values. Thirty years later (twenty of them spent in the effete East), he could say: "I think the most enjoyable thing in the world is to work with life itself. That's a criticism I've had of this whole century. It has worked with machines rather than with life."[13] For numerous reasons he cultivated the image of a dirt farmer, hair never combed, sheepishly awkward at social gatherings and political rallies. For many years Wallace was genuinely uncomfortable when forced to venture into big cities. He once wrote, for example, of the "nausea" that gripped him when surrounded by the "hordes" in the New York subway.

Believing in the primacy of agriculture (for both practical and philosophical reasons), Wallace was a great admirer of Thomas Jefferson. In many ways the awesome variety of Wallace's interests and endeavors during the 1920s—statistical analyses of the corn/hog ratio and the possible relationship between weather and crop yields, establishment of a hybrid seed company and participation in several other enterprises (including one to make plywood from cornstalks), editorship of *Wallaces' Farmer*, service in organizations such as the Stable Money League, and innumerable appearances at farmers' picnics and grange meetings on behalf of scientific farming, tariff reduction, and the McNary-Haugen bill—seem now almost a conscious effort to imitate the philosopher-statesman. Long afterwards he spoke of visiting Europe in 1929 and of seeing a scientific colleague, Professor Punnett, at Cambridge. "I talked with some of his fellow professors there and they criticized him very gravely on the score that he much preferred to play tennis than attend to his scientific knitting—which gave me a sort of fellow feeling for Punnett. I felt in those days the purpose of the world was to make it so stable that we could all spend our time gardening or taking care of a small amount of livestock or playing tennis."[14]

One may say that there was in the early years of Henry A. Wallace's editorial tenure a rather detached view of the problems confronting American agriculture. His proposed solutions, not surprisingly, were founded upon voluntarism. First, remove the protectionist tariffs that were choking world trade. Once Europe was permitted to sell its industrial and luxury goods at competitive prices in the American market, many of the dollars earned would be spent for the products of America's farms.[15] Second, farmers should demand "the moral, legal and economic equivalent of what the corporate form of organization gives to industry and union organization gives to labor."[16] Third, well, there really could be no third—no general solution—in that climate. Wallace, following the lead of his elders, advocated policing of railroad rates, tax revision, improved arrangements for agricultural financing, conservation, participation in cooperatives, and "Less Corn, More Clover, More Money," the famous slogan coined by *Wallaces' Farmer* to publicize *voluntary* control of production.[17]   Increasingly, however, as the postwar agricultural depression persisted and in some areas intensified, Henry A. Wallace began to look past the illusory willingness of farmers to cooperate and to consider government aid to agriculture. His concern at this time was entirely Iowa and farmers. "I was for agriculture first, last, and all the time," he later admitted. "I wasn't battling for either labor or business, except insofar as labor and business helped the farmer. It was a rather limited point of view, but in view of the fact that the farmers were getting it in the neck more than the others, I think it was probably justifiable at the time." But he also stressed: "I was in favor of any plan that would do the job for the farmers. I was completely eclectic—there wasn't anything doctrinaire with me."[18] That eclecticism led Wallace to assume a leading role in the battle to win approval for the McNary-Haugen bill, a scheme for agricultural relief which he and his father had helped to devise. In retrospect, it seems surprising that Henry A. would support so enthusiastically a measure that could be described as a "tariff for agriculture," since he abhorred protectionism of any kind for any reason. One way out of this apparent contradiction is to stress, as does Joan Hoff Wilson in *Herbert Hoover: Forgotten Progressive*, how "McNary-Haugenism . . . became one of the first steps in the direction of statist corporatism taken by New Deal agricultural reformers under the leadership of . . . Henry Agard Wallace."[19] This is certainly valid, though the distance between McNary-Haugenism and the later agricultural programs of the New Deal is so staggeringly great as to make their common point of origin appear essentially irrelevant.

The personal factor undoubtedly was extremely important. The death of his father (caused by an infected gall bladder complicated by exhaustion from overwork) in October, 1924, was a shattering blow to Henry A. Wallace. His grief focused on two matters. Acknowledging his father's quiet support of the McNary-Haugen proposal, Henry A. vowed to achieve the goal of federal assistance to agriculture, thereby vindicating, justifying, and memorializing the contributions of Henry C. Wallace as secretary of agriculture. The second commitment arose from Henry A.'s anguished conviction that Herbert Hoover (and to a lesser degree President Calvin Coolidge) were somehow directly responsible for his father's death.[20] This obsession, drawing upon the old, confused conflict between the Wallaces and Hoover over the latter's treatment of farmers (especially hog growers) during and just after the First World War, long bedeviled Henry A. Wallace.[21] It may be too much to state that he became active at the national level in the struggle to put over McNary-Haugenism (thereby acquiring a certain visibility and dealing with the remnants of the Progressive movement) only because Herbert Hoover was an early and vociferous opponent of McNary-Haugenism, production controls, and any sort of government aid for agriculture. But there is no doubt that Henry A. Wallace despised Hoover.

Direct and significant involvement in national politics dated from the period immediately after Henry C. Wallace's death. Predictably, Henry A. had voted for Robert LaFollette in 1924 out of spite. He took no part in the campaign. Indeed, he found it difficult to take seriously the *idea* of political affiliation, and thus the competition between political parties and the related organizational issues within parties never stirred his interest. "It's not my method of working—that's all," he later declared.[22] For that reason, he never became involved in the internecine strife between Progressives in Congress, though he respected George W. Norris and corresponded infrequently with other Progressive leaders.[23] Wallace did play an active role in the campaign to persuade Governor Frank Lowden to run for president as a third-party, progressive candidate. His point of view was that in a contest between Herbert Hoover and Al Smith "the farmer is . . . on the outside looking in. He didn't pick the candidates; he feels no special interest in either. There is no reason to get into a sweat over either one."[24]

Henry A. Wallace eventually endorsed Al Smith for the presidency in 1928 (though the public announcement came late in the campaign), and he did some speaking for the Democratic candidate (going to rallies with Milo Reno). But the reasons for supporting Smith were negative: his enmity for Hoover and a sense of hopelessness about the Republican party's position on agriculture. Even the 1932 campaign, during which Wallace spoke strongly for Franklin D. Roosevelt and served on the executive committee of the "National Progressive League," organized by independents and progressive Republicans for FDR, did not convert Wallace to a belief in partisan politics.[25] He was still very much committed to an agricultural perspective on national and international affairs. On the other hand, Wallace did not suffer the agonized doubts and ultimate disillusionment with Roosevelt and with the New Deal that was the lot of so many Progressives.[26]

3

The reasons for the easy transition to New Deal liberalism are several. Most obvious, Henry A. Wallace was never greatly interested in progressivism as a political movement. Thus the postmortems about "what might have been" had little meaning for him. Such observations as Justice Brandeis' epigram, "Europe was devastated by war, we by the aftermath," or the lament of William Allen White, "What a God-damned world this is! . . . If anyone had told me ten years ago that our country would be what it is today . . . I should have questioned his reason," were addressed to another, older audience.[27] Certainly Henry A. Wallace, in the years after 1928, had not "strayed into a confused and largely uncharted diaspora," as one historian has written of the Progressive movement as a whole.[28] He kept busy with various projects, especially the continuing crusade to secure "parity" for American agriculture. Having decided that the "Voluntary Domestic Allotment Plan"—a scheme for controlling agricultural production worked out by William J. Spillman, John D. Black, and M.L. Wilson—offered a solution to the problem of agricultural prices, Wallace quietly abandoned McNary-Haugenism and, from 1929 to 1933, devoted his efforts to the furtherance of the VDAP. As a result, he became identified as the chief advocate of the application of planning to agriculture, bridging a gulf between Veblen's institutional economics and the "freewheeling pragmatism" of the New Deal.[29]

Second, and perhaps most important, Wallace was not greatly affected by the crisis of confidence that engulfed so many Progressives after 1928 because he did not accept the views that produced it. To many Progressives, the debacles of 1926-1929, reflecting internal disorganization and conflict as well as external indifference to the cause, could be traced to a pervasive failure of leadership.[30] There continued to exist in Congress a group of able and influential congressmen who served, in the words of Senator Norris, as "a nucleus for the millions of progressives throughout the country who are not content to entrust their government to machine-ridden parties and monopoly-controlled bosses;" but this group was almost entirely western and basically concerned with regional issues.[31] No one appeared who possessed the vision and political skills to create a new, *national* synthesis between progressive values and the reality of an ethnically and racially diverse, urban, industrial nation. Indeed, many (most?) old-line Progressives concluded that positive leadership and progressivism, a movement founded on protest, were contradictory. Wallace himself ultimately became disenchanted with the movement ("It seems as though . . . Progressives are splendid critics but very poor builders," he observed in 1935), but he never lost faith in the potential for creative leadership.[32] The reason, in my opinion, was that the special religious convictions that by the late 1920s infused Henry A. Wallace's scientific and philosophical inquiries also shaped his political views.

Briefly stated, Wallace had by the late 1920s become deeply involved with various individuals and cults espousing mystical religious pathways. Having been raised a Presbyterian, he had left the church in 1913, when he was twenty-five. He was fascinated by the concerns of people such as William James (whose *Varieties of Religious Experience* he used as a Sunday school text) and admitted later that "in the years following my leaving the United Presbyterian Church I would say that I was probably a *practical* mystic." He was introduced to the writings of Madame Helena Blavatsky, the remarkable nineteenth-century feminist, explorer, and mystic who had founded the Theosophical Society, and Wallace pursued an interest in theosophy for the next decade. In the mid-1920s, again possibly because of the shock of his father's sudden death, Wallace even took the step of joining a theosophical offshoot, the Liberal Catholic Church. At the same time, he became engaged in a complex friendship with a self-proclaimed mystic and medicine man, Charles Roos. Subsequently, Wallace established a similarly intense relationship with the Russian artist, mystic, and charlatan, Nicolas P. Roerich.[33]

Thus is should be clear that Henry A.'s penchant for biblical references was not simply a Wallace family rhetorical trait. He could and did speak with confidence of the imminent coming of a great teacher (in modern parlance, "guru") who would also bring about the total reformation of society. Perhaps, he wrote in a 1928 column, a "Ghandi" [*sic*] would appear in the corn belt, and later he stated his belief that this new leader "has a doctrine which will furnish us the equivalent in terms of Christianity of what Ghandi has given to India."[34] In January, 1932, he observed: "Empires rise and pass away, and ours may pass, too, if leadership does not soon arise proportionate to the needs of the time.

I am confidently expecting such leadership, altho as yet no sign has appeared."[35] There is not time here to discuss Wallace's expectations about that leader and the signs that would herald the leader's arrival. Suffice it to say that for a time Franklin D. Roosevelt, the "flaming one," became that secular messiah, with Wallace as his first apostle. That particular conviction did not last. Indeed, when Wallace emerged from the tremendous political and personal testing to which he was subjected between 1933 and 1936, his enthusiasm for messiahs of any sort had been burned away. Gone, too, were the attachments to progressive tenets and values. There was still the belief that a cooperative commonwealth, now on a global scale, was feasible, but little was expressed about its specific features. What remained was a faith in humanity as much transcendentalist as progressive.

Henry A. Wallace's relationship to progressivism is hardly typical, though there were others who, like him, found solace "in making themselves better individuals" while awaiting the arrival of the dynamic leader. What is characteristic, perhaps, is his very intense and individualistic response to the problems of the day. Otis Graham has suggested that the Progressives might best be described as "a kind of secular clergy." If that insight is valid, then Henry A. Wallace, preaching the gospel of cooperation in his distinctive way, may well have been in the mainstream of progressivism.[36]

NOTES

1   *Wallaces' Farmer*, July 9, 1926; Donald Kirschner's article, "Henry A. Wallace as Farm Editor," *American Quarterly*, 18 (summer 1965), 187-202, provides a full discussion of Wallace's anti-urban views.

2   Henry A. Wallace, "Reminiscences," Columbia Oral History Collection, Columbia University, 49.

3   Russel B. Nye, *Midwestern Progressive Politics: A Historical Study of Its Origins and Development* (East Lansing, 1959), 288. The theme of the power of the state as the essential difference between progressivism and the New Deal is stressed by many scholars.

4   John M. Blum, ed., *The Price of Vision: The Diary of Henry A. Wallace, 1942-1946* (Boston, 1973), 14. Blum continues: "He cast himself often as a prophet or witness, now in the role of Joseph husbanding his people's resources, now as Micah beating swords into ploughshares, now as Gideon attacking a wicked citadel . . . . His was strongly a Social Gospel, but he tempered that gospel with a tenderness that displayed his natural charity." *Ibid.*, 14-15.

5   Russell Lord, *The Wallaces of Iowa* (Boston, 1947), 193. This remains the most insightful of all the biographical studies of Henry A. Wallace.

6   Blum, 10. Henry A. Wallace later admitted: "During the period from 1920 to 1930, I thought it was possible to get certain segments of the Republican and Democratic Parties to pull together. I wanted to work outside the scope of parties, and I wasn't interested in either party as a party . . . . I never felt completely at home in the Democratic Party . . . . At the same time,

I had found by experience what the Republican Party was." Wallace, "Reminiscences," 138, 5362.

7   Blum, 12. "Father and Grandfather . . . felt that Bryan was dangerously radical . . . although my grandfather was much more progressive than the ordinary Republican." Wallace, "Reminiscences," 6.

8   Henry Wallace, *Trusts and How to Deal with Them* (Des Moines, 1899), 5. Uncle Henry believed in regulation and not destruction. "The problem, therefore, of emasculating large aggregations of capital and destroying their power for evil while leaving their power for good unimpaired, is perhaps the greatest problem that has ever confronted the American people." *Ibid.*, 160. See also Norman D. Markowitz, *The Rise and Fall of the People's Century: Henry A. Wallace and American Liberalism, 1941-1948* (New York, 1973), 10-11.

9   Wallace, "Reminiscences," 120.

10   Blum, 8. Shortly after Thorstein Veblen's death, Wallace wrote: "One of the greatest men of his generation died early in August this year. His name was Thorstein Veblen and not one farmer in a thousand ever heard of him . . . . One hundred years from now people will read Veblen's books and realize that he was one of the few men of the early twentieth century who really knew what was going on." *Wallaces' Farmer*, Aug. 30, 1929.

11   Wallace, "Reminiscences," 5283-84. It is notable that he read verbatim into the oral history memoir those articles and editorials from *Wallaces' Farmer* he considered to be most important.

12   Thirty years later, Wallace said: "If I were to rewrite that editorial today, I wouldn't change any of it." *Ibid.*, 5284.

13   *Ibid.*, 5207. His fascination with the process of growth and development was a basic element in his personality. That led to anti-urban hostility. For example, he wrote in the early 1920s that it had been "proven" that families could not maintain their "vitality" in cities for more than three generations. "Put the third generation of a wild animal bred in the zoo up against an animal of the same species that has never left his native environment, and you will have a splendid demonstration of what effect unnatural surroundings can have on vitality." *Wallaces' Farmer*, April 14, 1922.

14   Henry A. Wallace, "Address to the Poultry Breeders Roundtable, Kansas City, Missouri, May 3, 1959," Henry A. Wallace Papers, Miscellany, in the author's possession.

15   Wallace's commitment to economic internationalism was extremely strong. "When we demand that the European countries pay up the money they owe us and at the same time raise our tariff, it is just like our having hold of the back of the neck with one hand pulling them towards us, and using a pitchfork against their belly with the other hand poking them away from us." He noted that he gave that speech at over one hundred picnics and meetings. Wallace, "Reminiscences," 122.

16   This is, of course, "parity." Wallace, "Reminiscences," 5275.

17   The slogan appeared on the masthead of *Wallaces' Farmer* beginning in 1923. He adopted almost verbatim the Progressive party platform of 1924. See *Wallaces' Farmer*, Feb. 3, 1922.

18   Wallace, "Reminiscences," 5275, 148. He observed later: "The farmers were increasingly getting around to the point of view . . . that the situation was so desperate that somebody had to do something. The only one they could think of was the government." *Ibid.*, 5343b.

19   Joan Hoff Wilson, *Herbert Hoover: Forgotten Progressive* (Boston, 1975), 105.

20   See Edward L. and Frederick H. Schapsmeier, *Henry A. Wallace of Iowa: The Agrarian Years, 1910-1940* (Ames, Ia., 1968), 79-80, and Lord, *Wallaces of Iowa*, 257-58.

21   Russell Lord has written: "By 1929 there still was talk among friends and partisans of the Wallace family depicting young Henry as a sort of brooding, scientific Hamlet, borne down by his father's death in the political-economic conflict." *Wallaces of Iowa*, 280.

22   Wallace, "Reminiscences," 131.

23   Note Leroy Ashby's assessment: "By the 1928 election, the progressive movement stood in shambles, the victim not only of postwar reaction and 'New Era' prosperity but also of cultural conflicts relating to values, morals, traditions, and personal liberties." *The Spearless Leader: Senator Borah and the Progressive Movement in the 1920's* (Urbana, Ill., 1972), 260. A tabulation of letters between Wallace and various Progressive leaders reveals the following for the period prior to 1933: LaFollette 2, Norris 6, Borah 21, Haugen 8, Lowden 15. Earl M. Rogers, ed., *The Wallace Papers: An Index*, 2 vols. (Iowa City, 1975).

24   *Wallaces' Farmer*, Sept. 28, 1928.

25   N.E. Kendall to Franklin D. Roosevelt, Nov. 15, 1932, Franklin D. Roosevelt Papers, OF 955, Franklin D. Roosevelt Library; Henry Morgenthau, Jr., to Franklin D. Roosevelt, May 5, 1932, FDR Gubernatorial Papers, Box 122, Morgenthau folder, Franklin D. Roosevelt Library. See also *Wallaces' Farmer*, Oct. 29, 1932.

26   An excellent analysis of this subject is Otis L. Graham's *An Encore for Reform: The Old Progressives and the New Deal* (New York, 1967).

27   Quoted in Alpheus T. Mason, *Brandeis: A Free Man's Life* (New York, 1946), 530; William Allen White to Ray Stannard Baker, Dec. 8, 1926, in Walter Johnson, ed., *Selected Letters of William Allen White, 1899-1943* (New York, 1947), 213.

28   Graham, 8.

29   An interesting characterization of the contrasts between the New Deal and progressivism is offered by Otis Graham: "The New Deal was distinguished by a political and moral style, by that freewheeling pragmatism and toughmindedness which set men like Harry Hopkins, Maury Maverick, and Tommy Corcoran apart from men like the Pinchots or Burton Wheeler or George Record." *Ibid.*, 8.

30   This argument is developed thoroughly in Ashby, *Spearless Leader*.

31   Richard Lowitt, *George W. Norris: The Persistence of a Progressive, 1913-1933* (Urbana, Ill., 1971), 414.

32   Henry A. Wallace, "Diary," Jan. 26, 1935, Henry A. Wallace Papers, University of Iowa Libraries.

33   Wallace, "Reminiscences," 49. References to theosophy are to be found in letters in the 1920s to Louis Bean, Milo Perkins, Mary Rumsey, and Daniel Wallace. Henry A. Wallace Papers, Boxes 1 and 2, University of Iowa Libraries. For Roerich, see Roerich Museum, *Roerich Museum, a Decade of Activity, 1921-1931* (New York, 1931), and Jean Duvernois, *Roerich: Biographical Fragments* (New York, 1932).

34   *Wallaces' Farmer*, Aug. 10, 1928.

35   *Wallaces' Farmer*, Jan. 23, 1932. "And he shall judge among many peoples, and rebuke strong nations afar off," Wallace proclaimed, citing Micah. *Wallaces' Farmer*, May 7, 1932.

36   Graham, 12-13; *Wallaces' Farmer*, Aug. 17, 1923.

COMMENTARY:
THREE PROGRESSIVES FROM IOWA

RICHARD LOWITT

IOWA'S CONTRIBUTION to the Progressive movement, however one wishes to define that term, is quite remarkable. The three representatives whose careers were just examined could be matched by many others. One thinks, for example, of the remarkable group of Grinnell graduates who made contributions to several major and minor New Deal programs, and of a larger group of Iowa State University graduates who staffed the United States Department of Agriculture, providing two Secretaries during the 1920s and 1930s, and who all in one way or another were involved in developing programs to assist agriculture in its time of trouble. One Iowa Progressive who has long interested me is William Peters Hepburn, not only for his role in sponsoring a measure granting effective authorization to the Interstate Commerce Commission to regulate railroad rates during Theodore Roosevelt's presidency, but also because, as far as I can determine, he was among the first, if not the first, member of Congress to champion curbing the power of the Speaker. Hepburn left Congress early in 1909, just as the Insurgency revolt was getting under way in earnest. But he more than anyone else might be properly called the godfather of that movement.

Nevertheless, despite an abundance of Iowa Progressives, it is not difficult to understand why our speakers examined the careers of Gilbert Haugen, Herbert Hoover, and Henry A. Wallace—their papers are housed in repositories in this vicinity: the State Historical Society, the Presidential Library at nearby West Branch, and the University of Iowa Libraries. While we have heard interesting and important papers from three outstanding scholars, it is worthwhile also to note that there are able scholars connected with one or the other of these institutions who have made or are making significant contributions to our understanding of these Iowa Progressives. We could just as easily—and certainly at less expense—have heard papers from them today. We have heard introductions from some of them. Perhaps we will hear comments from others, as soon as I get finished talking.

Richard Lowitt is Professor of History, Iowa State University.

While some among you might disagree with my calling William Peters Hepburn a Progressive, none, I think, will disagree with Professor Fite's characterization of Gilbert N. Haugen as a pragmatic Progressive. Fite establishes Haugen's credentials by delineating his efforts "to assure equal opportunity, to reduce economic exploitation, and to guarantee fair treatment to all." To achieve this goal Haugen supported the reform legislation of the Theodore Roosevelt presidency as well as the Insurgency revolt during the Taft administration. Professor Fite, obviously, devotes most of his attention to Haugen's efforts to assist agriculture. Like a vast number of Americans in his day with roots in rural America or with strong ties to various rural areas in Europe, Haugen was an agricultural fundamentalist, a view that seems strange to many at the present time. Yet this premise helped give meaning to Haugen's career as well as to his life. And it perhaps can help explain what Professor Fite suggests as possible departures from the progressive fold by Haugen, namely, his opposition to postal savings, parcel post, federal guarantee of bank deposits, and his failure to support Theodore Roosevelt in 1912.

As a prominent and successful banker in Northwood, Iowa, his opposition to postal savings is understandable, as is his opposition to federal guarantee of bank deposits, though this was a complicated and technical issue which I do not have the time to fully unravel at present. More important, his opposition to parcel post does make sense from the viewpoint of a Progressive and agricultural fundamentalist. Parcel post assisted in the destruction of small-town mid-America, in that it tremendously aided mail order houses in Chicago and elsewhere in their endeavors to serve rural America. Parcel post made the lot of independent Main Street businessmen more difficult and assisted the process, already well under way, of breaking down a sense of community and of tying the farmer more closely to distant business interests. Soon these interests would have their own representatives on Main Street, either replacing or hiring the small independent businessmen who largely served rural customers.

As far as sticking with Taft in 1912, Iowa Progressives, like those in Nebraska and elsewhere in this part of the country, faced a terrible dilemma. Iowa Progressives had worked hard and long to capture control of the Republican party from the standpatters and the Old Guard. Then, in August of 1912, with state and local campaigns already under way, Theodore Roosevelt asked them to join his third party crusade, in effect to turn the Republican party organization back to the very group they had recently wrested it from. Most Iowa Progressives, like those in Nebraska and neighboring states, agreed with Haugen and reluctantly endorsed Taft while concentrating on state races and the progressive records of the Iowa Republican candidates. It is interesting to note that in 1912 Wilson carried Iowa, Nebraska, Kansas, and several other midwestern states where progressive Republicans dominated the party machinery. In many of these states the political situation was so tense that the

Progressive party was unable to field a full ticket. Indeed, it was less represented in the Midwest, the home of progressive Republicanism, than in any other part of the nation. Haugen's attitude in 1912 is understandable—and it was echoed by many other progressive Republican candidates in that exciting election year.

But it was his concern for the plight of agriculture in the 1920s, when he chaired the House Agriculture Committee, that brought Haugen to national prominence and to the attention of historians. Scholars, when they examine party politics on the national level in the 1920s, usually focus on the Democratic party as the one on the verge of disintegration, beset by strife and tensions that threatened to tear it apart. In doing so they let the Republican party off too easily. It, too, was beset by strife and tensions. An incumbent president twice vetoing a major measure approved by a majority of the members of his own party in Congress is a rare occurrence, as is a Republican congress turning down a cabinet nominee of a Republican president. Yet these phenomena and others all occurred during the Coolidge administration. Perhaps it is because the future of American politics resided in urban America, and historians eager to exploit new areas and new research techniques found it more profitable and more interesting to examine the dimensions of the Democratic decline. Whatever the reason, less attention has been focused on the Republican party and its tensions in the 1920s.

Professor Fite in his paper succinctly discusses one of the major controversies dividing the Republican party: that pertaining to agriculture. And it is at this point that the three Iowa Progressives discussed today come together. All were Republicans whose fate in part was determined by the plight of agriculture. Henry Wallace, who had left his party by 1928, joined the New Deal and helped develop a new approach to the plight of agriculture. Herbert Hoover, who said he had an effective answer to the farm problem, went down to defeat in part because his solution did not work, and he dragged Gilbert Haugen, whose bill never had a chance because of presidential opposition, down with him. In 1928, as Professor Fite notes, Haugen favored Frank Lowden, as did most leading farm spokesmen in Iowa. Leland Sage in his *History of Iowa* observes that "Iowa farm leaders remembered Hoover's solid opposition to McNary-Haugenism and his favoritism for industry, and therefore opposed his nomination."[1] Most of them, however, endorsed Hoover in the national campaign and they paid dearly for it. In 1928 Haugen ran unopposed in his district; the Democrats were unable to field a candidate against him. In 1932 Haugen failed to carry a single county in his district. And within a year he was dead.

Yet as Professor Fite observes, his career did not truly end in failure. The Agricultural Adjustment Act sought the same objective as the McNary-Haugen bills. *Wallaces' Farmer,* for August 5, 1933, stated: "the spirit of the McNary-Haugen bill is the spirit of the present farm act. Both aim at raising farm incomes. The long agitation for the McNary-Haugen bill helped generally to prepare the farmer and the public for the more radical and thorough going program now underway."[2] Professor Theodore Wilson makes the same point by quoting Professor Joan Hoff Wilson's biography of Herbert Hoover in his paper.

However, Hoover, as secretary of commerce, strongly opposed the McNary-Haugen bill, and as an ex-president he just as strongly opposed the AAA and other New Deal farm programs, as Professor Wilson notes in her paper. Until recently Hoover's views were rarely taken seriously by historians, who in varying degrees regarded his career as a failure. Within the past two decades renewed interest in his career, while it has not reversed the verdict of failure with regard to the Hoover presidency, has enormously expanded our knowledge and understanding of both the man and his times. How does one explain this renewed interest, the increased publication of articles and books, the growing number of doctoral dissertations, the mounting frequency of sessions and meetings devoted to Herbert Hoover? The answers, most obviously, lie close by—the availability of Hoover Library with its rich resources beckoning scholars, the work of Professor Ellis Hawley and his able and industrious graduate students, the well-received and important books of Professor Joan Hoff Wilson—all have expanded our knowledge and understanding of Herbert Hoover and the controlling framework of ideas that guided his career. Other scholars have added their mite—and the work of all these scholars have already influenced what writers of textbooks and classroom teachers are saying about Herbert Hoover. But there is, I think, something further involved in the rehabilitation of Herbert Hoover now under way.

Hoover, as president, was caught in the vortex of the second momentous failure that engulfed the United States, which until recently was universally regarded as the greatest success story in recorded history. The first time America failed was in the 1860s, when its vaunted political system disintegrated and was unable to stave off the crisis of secession, thereby allowing the nation to indulge in the luxury of killing over one-half million of its ablest younger citizens while the rest of the world stood by, something that could not have happened elsewhere in the nineteenth century. In the late 1920s when its renowned economic system collapsed, America for the second time in its history experienced failure, and Hoover, rightly or wrongly, served as convenient scapegoat. Indeed, given his reputation as an engineer and as a humanitarian, Hoover came to symbolize America's failure as unemployed and dispossessed citizens gave his name to the ramshackle communities that sprang up in almost every metropolitan area. The third time America failed as a nation is at the present time, with its involvement in southeast Asia, with the Nixon presidency, with the erosion of moral integrity on the part of leaders who thought nothing of lying to the American people and making devious decisions and commitments which we are still learning about at the present time. Given these circumstances, many citizens, including numerous scholars—besides asking questions, protesting, and criticizing—began to frame their arguments within consciously articulated ideological constructs calling for a diminished role of government and an increasing sense of community. I think it is within this context that the revival of interest in Herbert Hoover is growing by leaps and bounds. Scholars, who, more than ever before, are showing an increased interest in ideology, now find Hoover a provocative and exciting figure. He had a conscious ideology. He did not believe in expanding the role of government. And he favored cooperation without binding commitments at home and abroad, something that people on both the left and right fringes of the political spectrum, where ideologies usually are most consciously pronounced, find enticing. Thus we now have an historic personage praised more for what he did *not* do than for what he did.

This renewed interest, nevertheless, has benefited all of us. Thanks to it, we now have a much better understanding of aspects of twentieth-century American history: of an organizational approach to decision-making in both the private and public sector, an approach which rejected both *laissez faire* and government management (at least Hoover wished it to avoid management); an approach which was acceptable to a democratic nation and which seemingly would continue to offer opportunities for people and business enterprises of all kinds. The terminology occasionally differs: "corporate liberalism," "associationism," "welfare capitalism as opposed to welfare statism" are some of the terms that have been used to explain this development. But whatever the term, Herbert Hoover's career adds to our understanding, and in many ways it is central to this development, particularly in the decade of the 1920s. In the first part of her paper Professor Wilson carefully delineates the framework in which Hoover approached this theme. In the 1930s, however, government played a larger role, and while Hoover continually criticized his successor and shifted his emphasis, his belief in an organizational system stressing cooperation and sharing between economic and other units in the social order, with government assisting and disseminating information, did not diminish. Hoover's ideology did not call for government playing an active role in this voluntary process—except in periods of dire emergency, and then only on a temporary basis. During the 1920s a handful of corporate liberals were willing to go further than Hoover and have businessmen cooperate with bureaucrats in developing policies in which government would play a dominant role in efforts to balance and harmonize the functioning of the American economy. In the early 1930s their numbers increased, and they eagerly cooperated with New Dealers in their efforts to revive American business.

Professor Wilson devotes her attention to Hoover's response to these developments. That Hoover would be in opposition of course could be taken for granted. The very important point that she makes is that in opposing the early New Deal, Hoover shifted his arguments from a stress on "corporate liberalism" to a base predicated upon "moral rationalization" and that in doing so he remained well within the progressive fold. She indicates, following Otis Graham, that many old line Progressives found themselves in opposition to the New Deal.[3] She makes an additional point that, previously, Hoover's progressive career had been based almost exclusively on "compulsive activism." I have some difficulty in accepting this point: for example, I find it hard to find "compulsive activism" in his presidency after 1929, when he secured the legislative program he thought would put America on a sound, rational, and prosperous economic base.

Many years ago Richard Hofstadter, I believe in *The Age of Reform*, made the penetrating point that in the 1930s there occurred a basic reversal of roles between the parties. Previously, throughout the late nineteenth and early twentieth centuries, it was the Democrats who talked about principles, challenges to liberty and freedom, basic violations of rights, subverting the constitution, etc. In the 1930s the Republicans assumed that role, while Democrats became the movers and the shakers.[4] Professor Wilson indicates that Hoover played a prominent, if not the leading, role in formally launching this principled attack, with the publication of *The Challenge to Liberty* in 1934.

What is missing from her account of Hoover's analysis, despite his collecting statistical data and talk of conspiracy and various "isms"—and here Hofstadter again comes to mind, with his discussion of the paranoid personality—is any mention of the plight of the country, with millions of unemployed; with actual starvation owing to the collapse of private charities; with the human dimensions of a collapsed economy in the industrial, financial, and agricultural sectors; with a situation in many areas, including several places in Iowa, that was turning ugly and violent. It was this situation, of course, that accounted for Hoover's defeat in 1932—and it was this situation that many New Dealers, as pragmatic progressives, sought to cope with in an abundance of contradictory, confusing, inefficient ways that, despite what one might think of them, were astoundingly successful in the only arena that really matters to anyone engaged in mainstream party politics, namely, the ballot box. And Hoover, now reverting to moral criticism, faced the same problem he faced as president in calling for voluntary cooperative action, namely, he could never adequately convey a clear picture of what he was about. To be sure, the times were against him, and, as Professor Wilson suggests in her concluding statement, Hoover's views "in perceiving the significant structural and attitudinal differences between the New Era and the New Deal . . . possibly seems more important for the 1970s than [they] did for the 1930s."

Most twentieth-century American presidents, upon leaving office, usually devote their time to preparing their memoirs or accounts of their tenure: explaining, rationalizing, defending the programs and policies they pursued while in office. Hoover had others—William Starr Meyers, Walter Newton,

Arthur Hyde—do this for him. He did not publish his memoirs for another two decades, preferring instead to continue the barrage of moral criticism set forth in *The Challenge to Liberty* with eight volumes of *Addresses upon the American Road* and other works, thereby insuring that posterity would have relatively easy access to his views.

Interesting also is the point I suggested earlier, that many corporate liberals went beyond Hoover in the 1930s and sought to realize some of his goals by working within the New Deal, to seek through NRA and other programs the rational, orderly, harmonious, and balanced goals for the American economy that Hoover desired. As Professor Ellis Hawley and others have noted, Hoover by the end of his presidency, instead of leading in the search for these goals, had become a deterrent to realizing them.[5] And by and large he remained such when he shifted the basis of his critique and became morally indignant and increasingly negative in attitude.

Now for several minor points or observations. In preparing for publication a diary located in the library at Iowa State University, I gained an insight as to how Hoover was hoisted on his own petard. His concern for efficiency and gathering statistical data and information of all kinds relating to the functioning of the economy created serious problems for him during his presidency, since all economic indicators and statistical data released by various departments and agencies reinforced the dramatic decline of the economy. Hoover saw one of the prime techniques he encouraged in government being used to discredit his administration and to further demoralize the American people. Nils Olsen, who was chief of the Bureau of Agricultural Economics, recorded in his diary an attempt by Hoover to prevent the release of at least one set of agricultural statistics relating to crop forecasts.

The same diary presents some tantalizing insights into a point that Professor Wilson makes in her valuable brief biography of Herbert Hoover, namely, that we know very little about him as a private person and that we will know little until the papers of his wife, Lou Henry, are open to the public. Other authors make a similar point. By themselves, Olsen's entries indicate nothing of great significance, though possibly they can suggest points that future researchers might be alerted to, in that they occasionally touch upon themes (racial attitudes and the role of women) that command attention at the present time. Olsen's diary recounts how Olsen and Arthur Hyde, the secretary of agriculture, became close friends. Soon Hyde was informing Olsen not only of his increasing doubts about Hoover's policies—to which the secretary nevertheless remained steadfastly loyal—but also, at times, of incidents and comments touching upon personal relations with the president. Two of the entries excerpted below center on such revelations from Secretary Hyde. The first is from Olsen's entry of September 3, 1929:

> During our visit the Secretary made the interesting comment that Rapidan was helping to loosen up the President socially to quite a degree. [Hoover

had a retreat on the Rapidan River in the Blue Ridge Mountains of Virginia.] He was now finding it possible to unbend and tell stories with the rest of them. The night before they sat around and told Negro stories for a couple of hours. The President himself told two or three which seemed to be real evidence of mellowing on his part.[6]

The second is from Olsen's entry of December 14, 1931:

The Secretary went on to remark that H. H. somehow had the way of saying the wrong thing and he clearly indicated that the situation now seemed hopeless. "You know," he said, "he has a childlike faith in statements and I think his actions grow out of a natural timidity to strike out, and also out of a compromising policy which has brought him where he is today." Then the Secretary told me how last Thursday (December 10) following the diplomatic dinner at the White House the cabinet members with their wives had adjourned to the President's quarters for refreshments. As that little party broke up the President tapped Hyde on the shoulder and asked him to step in to his office. Hyde said his heart sank into his boots, thinking that he would have to listen to some more of these hopeless statements to which H. H. was given. When he stepped in he found [Secretary of War] Pat Hurley there and the situation looked no better, but in the course of another half minute [Postmaster General] Walter Brown stepped in and he then thought things looked interesting and, sure enough, H. H. trotted out his twelve points on cooperation which he read in his simple childlike way. Hyde went on to say that the statement came out considerably modified from the original draft. He said that in commenting upon it to the President he said "The statement is all right. It is merely nailing to the mast the statement, but the trouble is that the foundation is defective so why nail it to the mast?"

A third excerpt, from Olsen's entry of December 9, 1932, describes a visit paid him that day by Ray Tucker, a prominent Washington correspondent who had covered the recent presidential election campaign:

Tucker has an intense antipathy for Hoover and said that his attitude was, to quite a degree, that of the press in general. As illustrations of this attitude, he referred to a number of episodes. For example, he referred to the inability of Hoover to take defeat on anything. He said the election was undoubtedly crushing to him. As an illustration of that he referred to the secret service which was guarding the President. A secret service man (whose name I have forgotten) assigned as the President's close bodyguard on his trip back to Washington from Palo Alto, said that at various stopping places the President shook hands with people and he was so absent minded that he did not realize he had shaken hands with his own bodyguard three times on the same occasion. When he was about to shake hands with him the fourth time, the bodyguard said, "Mr. President." The President then looked up and realized he had been shaking hands with the secret service man. The secret service man put his hand on the President's shoulder and told him he was mighty sorry for what had happened and cheered him up, and that with probably a lot of other influences sought [*sic*] of mellowed him and when he arrived at Washington he seemed more human than ever before. Tucker also told me about the picture taking episode at Palo Alto at the time of the President's nomination when Mrs. Hoover, who thinks she is an artist in the photographic field, stepped out and tried to tell the camera boys that their perspective was not right and that the group was not as it should be, and so forth and so on until the President finally lost his temper and said "That will do. You may go into the house." The press men's antipathy seems to have gone out against Mrs. Hoover too. As an illustration of that they have realized that she is uncomfortable about the spread between her front teeth and whenever she poses for a photograph she has her mouth shut but the boys fool her by clicking their camera and then she smiles and they then take the picture, spread and all. He also told me that when Mrs. Hoover began learning to ride horseback, instructions had gone out saying that no photographs should be taken until she had learned to ride her horse. The boys then concealed themselves in the bushes around the White House and when she was not looking, they got their photographs.

Henry A. Wallace succeeded Arthur Hyde as secretary of agriculture. Wallace, along with other New Dealers in the department, had little sympathy or liking for Hoover and his voluntary associational approach. Professor Theodore Wilson makes the point that Wallace personally "despised Hoover." The New Dealers were convinced that Hoover's approach had no relevance for the distressing situation engulfing American agriculture. Indeed, Wallace's father, secretary of agriculture under Harding, had previously reached a similar conclusion. What Hoover, as secretary of commerce, was doing to build his department as an efficient agency to serve the needs of American business, Henry C. Wallace was duplicating in the Department of Agriculture. Both men organized new bureaus, staffed them with experts, stressed the necessity for statistical data, and sought to provide new scientific and technical services designed to assist their respective clienteles. Wallace, however, was ready to have government play a more active role in directly assisting farmers in their efforts to secure their costs of production and to maintain a significant place in American life. Needless to say, the men disliked one another. And this also applied to most of their loyal bureau chiefs in their respective departments. Wallace's death in 1924 created a vacuum in the Department of Agriculture as far as active and open opposition to Hoover's views and developing programs to meaningfully cope with the farm problem were concerned.

Henry A. Wallace's entrance into the department helped change this situation. With the AAA, government sought to restrict production through the domestic allotment plan in an effort to promote parity for American agriculture. And Wallace's efforts, assisted by severe drought, succeeded far better than other early New Deal programs. But Wallace at the outset had no easy time of it. Confusion, controversy, and even chaos prevailed in the department as New Dealers battled one another, as top personnel were shifted to newly created action agencies, leaving long-term bureau chiefs to carry out their missions with smaller staffs. These chiefs were distressed and occasionally outraged by the arrogance and extreme views of some of Wallace's top personnel. Wallace was aware of all of this and more. He confided to his diary early in February, 1935, remarks that would have delighted Hoover. He wrote, "In this administration, the objectives are experimental and not clearly stated; therefore, there is certain to be, from the White House down, a certain amount of what seems to be intrigue. I do not think this situation will be remedied until the President abandons ... his experimental and somewhat concealed approach. There are ... many advantages to this approach but it does not lead to the happiest personal relationships and the best administration."[7]

Yet Wallace worked hard at reorganizing the department, turning it into an efficient and cohesive entity capable of assisting American agriculture in meeting its multi-faceted problems. Milton Eisenhower, who entered the department in the Coolidge administration, remarked that during the 1930s the USDA achieved the best administrative organization in Washington.[8] And the director of research for the President's Committee on Administrative Management concluded in 1937 that the department under Wallace gave greater attention to broad economic problems and made greater use of economists as advisors to the secretary than any other department.[9]

What is quite remarkable about all of this, as Professor Theodore Wilson amply illustrates in his paper, is that Wallace, though not lacking in ideas, was so short on practical administrative experience. He was a loner, with strong religious and mystical inclinations, a utopian with "a rather detached view of the problems confronting American agriculture." Yet at the same time he was clearly a Progressive, proclaiming with moral fervor "his very intense and individualistic response to the problems of the day." He also was a practical scientist and a student of Thorstein Veblen, Herbert Croly, John Dewey, Richard Ely, and Charles Beard. Like these and other Progressives, he was acutely aware of the necessity of social, economic, and political institutions' keeping pace with the progress of science and technology. He agreed with Herbert Hoover in calling for "a society that would need scientists and managers to fashion an abundant life for the common man." Like Hoover, he stressed statistical analysis. He went further and used both his scientific and statistical knowledge to establish successful business enterprises, though he never took an active role in their management. But he was interested in the managerial goals of order, stability, harmony, and balance. As Professor Theodore Wilson writes, in his early years "his proposed solutions, not surprisingly, were founded upon voluntarism." And, again like Hoover, as Professor Wilson further observes, he was "sheepishly awkward at social gatherings and political rallies."

That such a person should become our greatest secretary of agriculture and an outstanding administrator is little short of amazing. Add to this the fact that Rex Tugwell early in the New Deal confided to his diary his conviction that Wallace had presidential ambitions and that those ambitions animated his behavior from the outset of his tenure.[10] Parallels with Hoover's career in the 1920s immediately come to mind. A most interesting chapter in the biography that Professor Wilson is preparing certainly will be the one explaining Henry Wallace's shift from an aloof, pragmatic Progressive espousing a "very intense and individualistic response to the problems of the day" to one cast in the mold of corporate liberalism, taking up where his father left off.

In this respect, like Hoover, Wallace believed in planning. But unlike Hoover, Wallace attempted to translate the planning undertaken by the Bureau of Agricultural Economics, which in 1938 was designated as the planning agency in the department, into programs carried out by the Farm Security Administration, the Soil Conservation Service, and other action agencies connected with the department. Though Hoover denounced Wallace's programs, Wallace, like Hoover, was unable to satisfactorily resolve the critical problems of distribution and underconsumption. Indeed, he never sought to develop an alternative to the market price system of capitalism, endeavoring instead to raise agricultural prices, an effort in which he, unlike Hoover, was partially successful. Though their methods differed, both men sought similar goals.

Wallace, however, did not stop at this point. His progressivism went beyond concern for efficient bureaucratic management and encompassed a genuine regard for involving agricultural producers in decision making as it affected the land they farmed and the crops they produced. With broader responsibility placed upon the Department of Agriculture by Congress, Wallace was anxious that a method be devised for keeping the administrative processes as democratic as possible. Thus the Agricultural Adjustment Administration was established with committees in every county in the United States. The Farm Security Administration placed responsibility upon county committees for several phases of its activities, such as the tenant purchase program. And by the end of 1938, land-use planning committees were being organized in every farm state and county in the country. In these and other programs Wallace helped realize one of the early prominent progressive goals—that of more direct democracy, what Professor Wilson calls his "faith in humanity." In addition, these policies helped further a theme first suggested in a seminal piece of twentieth-century domestic legislation, the Reclamation Act of 1902, which expanded the concept of federalism by providing that the national government would help people—western water-users, under the terms of the Reclamation Act—to help themselves. President Eisenhower initially called such programs "creeping Socialism." He later expressed amazement when he learned that irrigation farmers were repaying the federal government for funds extended to their associations. In reality, this approach, I think, represented one of the more notable achievements of early twentieth-century Progressives, and Wallace helped expand it during the New Deal in his efforts to provide equality for agriculture.

Consequently, the Department of Agriculture, as already suggested, tried to establish in every farm community groups that could discuss the trend of events as they affected the general economy and agriculture in particular. These groups were encouraged to offer suggestions as to how programs could be more effective. They also were asked to set forth adjustments required for their locality, and at least 50 per cent of the people in a community were required to participate. At the county level the findings and objectives of the community were brought together into a county program. At this point community chairmen "reasoned" with county administrators of various agricultural programs. Elected county officials usually sat in on these meetings and participated in the resolution of some of the problems.

This process then continued on the state level, involving the administrative heads of all Department of Agriculture agencies. This group tried to work out policies and priorities for the operation of state programs, and efforts were made to involve state experiment stations as well as people in extension work and at the state colleges. While Hoover gathered statistics indicating the waste, confusion, and contradictions in the AAA, Wallace was achieving one of his progressive goals in two ways: *one* was casting administration in the Department of Agriculture within a democratic framework by decentralizing as far as current experience would then permit; the *other* was to encourage a formulation of policy at the grass roots, thereby fostering a new sense of community, again within a democratic framework.

Wallace, while primarily involved with farm programs, was also aware that only half of the farm problem was to be found on the farm. His progressivism went beyond rural fundamentalism. He recognized that farmers had a responsibility to urban consumers and that their livelihood depended upon consumer purchasing power. The paradox of want in the midst of plenty gravely disturbed him and, as a physical scientist as well as a progressive reformer, he was concerned that ways be worked out to provide better nutrition for families unable to purchase adequate food at market prices. Two of the devices inaugurated to meet this responsibility are still operative today: the food stamp program (dropped in 1943 but revised and resumed in the 1960s) and the school lunch program. And by the war period he carried his progressivism one step further and was considering broad international programs to combat world hunger, proclaiming them with both moral and mystical fervor.

Wallace clearly understood, as he remarked in 1961, that "only in agriculture is it definitely certain that we shall remain superior to the rest of the world for many years to come."[11] It was his hope that agricultural programs and policies would remain within the context and scope of the broad-gauged progressive approach that he launched as secretary of agriculture in the 1930s.

Three Progressives from Iowa—one a pragmatic Progressive, another a somewhat flexible ideological Progressive, the third a Progressive whose progressivism his biographer has some difficulty in defining, settling at present for a definition encompassing "a faith in humanity as much transcendentalist as progressive." All left their mark upon the American scene in the 1920s and 1930s. And the latter two continue to exert a significant influence upon American life today as well.

NOTES

1   Leland Sage, *History of Iowa* (Ames, 1974), 269.

2   Quoted in *Dictionary of American Biography*, 1958 ed., XI, Pt. 1, Supplement One, "Haugen, Gilbert Nelson," by Earle D. Ross, 385.

3   Otis L. Graham, Jr., *An Encore for Reform: The Old Progressives and the New Deal* (New York, 1967).

4   Richard Hofstadter, *The Age of Reform: From Bryan to F.D.R.* (New York, 1955). See the section entitled "The New Departure" in chap. VII, 300-314.

5   See the essay by Ellis Hawley in Joseph Huthmacher and Warren I. Susman, eds., *Herbert Hoover and the Crisis of American Capitalism* (Cambridge, Mass., 1973), 25-26.

6   For an analysis of Hoover's views on race see George F. Garcia, "Herbert Hoover and the Issue of Race," *Annals of Iowa*, 44 (winter 1979), 507-15.

7   Entry for February 3, 1935, as quoted in John M. Blum, ed., *The Price of Vision: The Diary of Henry A. Wallace, 1942-1946* (Boston, 1973), 18.

8   Richard S. Kirkendall, *Social Scientists and Farm Politics in the Age of Roosevelt* (Columbia, Mo., 1966), 231.

9   *Ibid.*, 163.

10   Rexford G. Tugwell, *Roosevelt's Revolution: The First Year—A Personal Perspective* (New York, 1977), 198-99, 206-208, 298-99.

11   Henry A. Wallace, *The Department As I Have Known It*, an address in the Centennial Lecture Series, U.S. Department of Agriculture (Nov. 1, 1961), 13-14. Copy in Wayne Darrow Papers, Special Collections, Iowa State University Library.

THE IOWA PROGRESSIVE TRADITION AND NATIONAL ACHIEVEMENTS

FRANK FREIDEL

IOWA, long famed for its tall corn, succulent pork, and well-marbled beef, also deserves acclaim for the notable and lasting contributions of several Iowans to modern America. Through the careers of three particularly outstanding figures one can examine something of the influence of their Iowa progressive origins upon their later views of the relationship between the federal government and the economy, especially agriculture, and toward enhancing the security and well-being of the American people. There is much in the Iowa roots of these leaders that illuminates their policies.

Iowa has not been a focal point of attention in national studies of progressivism, perhaps because of its averageness. The shaping of federal agricultural policy is a prime example. Historians of the agrarianism of the late nineteenth and twentieth centuries have concentrated upon the desperately impoverished states rather than Iowa, with its relative prosperity. During the late nineteenth century, unlike the Kansas following of the Populist "Mother" Lease, the Iowans raised more corn and less hell. In 1932-1933, Milo Reno and the Farmer's Holiday Association did something to change that image, but not for very long. Actually, it was the very fact that Iowa was the heartland of family-sized commercial farms, whose owners combined in farm organizations which could exercise the greatest political clout, that made the state so important. Agricultural economists of Iowa origins played a preponderant role in establishing and administering the federal policies of crop controls which wrought a revolution in national farm policy nearly a half-century ago.

The averageness of Iowa is significant in a broader view of progressivism. In a century of urbanization, it was in no danger of being swallowed by an expanding megalopolis. Those who love the state wince at the slurs of the trend setters on both the East and West coasts, their misuse of Keokuk and Dubuque as synonyms for less advanced taste in architecture or motion pictures. (Recently, of course, the locus of such remarks has shifted a little eastward, out of the state: "Will it play in Peoria?") What is to the point, the communities

Frank Freidel is Charles Warren Professor of American History, Harvard University.

of Iowa are so typical that sociologists wishing to survey national trends have long found they could best examine Cedar Rapids, which (along with Decatur, Illinois, and the more famous Muncie, Indiana, of "Middletown" fame) serves for sampling the tastes and interests of all Americans. To sneer at Dubuque is to ridicule all of middle-class America.

Iowa was typical of prosperous, progressive, rural America, with its small towns and cities dotting one of the world's most productive farming areas. It is representative of both middle-class and agrarian progressivism. That aspect was conspicuous during the progressive years, and later in the writings a generation ago of historians like George Mowry, a one-time professor at the University of Iowa. Solidly middle-class Iowa, free from excesses of poverty and wealth, came close to being the embodiment of the progressive ideal. I would not underestimate the significance of the progressivism of large cities, a vital part of the whole, but in recent years historians have focused upon it so pervasively that they have more than shifted the perspective. The time has come to look back at the kind of progressivism that flourished in Iowa.

Progressivism is such a many-faceted phenomenon that, as Joan Hoff Wilson reminds us, it encompassed a wide variety of twentieth-century political manifestations. It was the effort of the American people to perfect their government as an instrument to bring a larger measure of democracy and a greater degree of social and economic equity. It was optimistic and moral, attuned to a faith in an abundance expanding through the operation of the existing economic system, once it had been purified of its imperfections. It was based four-square on American traditions, especially those of individual freedom and self-reliance, and was opposed to those distant aggregations of power threatening to overturn these traditions. If this definition is vague and incomplete, so was progressivism. It was less consistent than pragmatic. I myself shall try to be pragmatic, to examine three remarkable national leaders who grew up in the Iowa progressive tradition as a means of coming to a clearer view of that tradition and what it meant in later decades.

Just to name the figures, Herbert Hoover, Henry A. Wallace, and Harry Hopkins, is to indicate something of the diversity within Iowa progressivism. No doubt the association of these three under the same rubric is enough to cause some indignation among adherents of one or the other, the feeling that Wallace or Hopkins was too radical or Hoover too conservative to include. Yet all three belong, and each in his thought owed a good bit to Iowa. All were eminent men who contributed much to this nation and the world. All have been the subject of biographies in recent years, and will be the subject of further, projected biographies in the next few years. They well deserve attention and, whether or not they would have thought so, merit association as heirs to the Iowa progressive tradition.

Senior and preeminent among the three was Herbert Hoover, born in West Branch in 1874. He spent only his earliest years in Iowa; orphaned, he was sent on an immigrant train to Oregon when he was eleven. He made his fortune as an international mining engineer and administrator while he was still a young man, and, with the outbreak of World War I, turned to public service. He became chairman of the Commission for Relief in Belgium, then of the Food Administration. During the 1920s, as secretary of commerce, he was the most innovative figure in Washington. In 1928 he was overwhelmingly elected president, but within a year a stock market crash signaled the onset of the Great Depression. Again Hoover was innovative in trying to combat the depression, but his policies did not work very well and his popularity dwindled. He lost the 1932 election decisively to Franklin D. Roosevelt.

Into the New Deal Roosevelt brought the two other Iowans, Henry A. Wallace and Harry Hopkins. Wallace, born in Adair County in 1888, of a family of farm editors and leaders, attended Iowa State and became an agricultural economist and plant breeder. In the 1920s, when his father was Harding's secretary of agriculture, Wallace was editor of the family farm paper, seeking the national crop controls Hoover opposed. Although still nominally a Republican, Wallace became Roosevelt's secretary of agriculture. He obtained crop controls for the primary benefit of commercial farmers, then gradually, as the New Deal progressed, became a champion of the underprivileged. As vice president, during World War II, he was the prime exponent of liberal New Deal policies, which he wished to apply internationally as well as within the United States. As the Cold War developed, he championed more friendly relations with the Soviet Union, breaking with the Truman administration and in 1948 running as the candidate of a third party, which he labelled "Progressive."

Hopkins, born in Sioux City in 1890, after graduating from Grinnell College went into settlement house work in New York City, and soon became a key welfare and urban health executive. He headed Roosevelt's relief programs, first in New York State and then, when the New Deal began, in Washington. Late in the New Deal he served as secretary of commerce, and in World War II won his greatest fame as Roosevelt's close adviser and personal emissary on diplomatic and military planning missions.

All three of these men shared a number of common characteristics, attributable in part to the times in which they grew up and in part to the Iowa location. (Of course, much of the influence of Iowa was not of a sort unique in this state.) There were many important differences among them in both personality and conviction, and even sharp antagonisms between Hoover on the one hand and Wallace and Hopkins on the other. These differences and antagonisms make more interesting the points in common.

First of all, there were the roots in the Iowa soil, with their connotations. The opening idyllic pages of Herbert Hoover's memoirs, written in 1915-1916 during periods of waiting while he was shuttling back and forth between wartime England and Belgium, are evocative of the values that Henry Nash Smith has delineated so skillfully in *Virgin Land*. Hoover's first lines are classic:

"I prefer to think of Iowa as I saw it through the eyes of a ten-year-old boy. Those were eyes filled with the wonders of Iowa's streams and woods, of the mystery of growing crops." One summer while he was living in Sioux County with an uncle who was "breaking in a prairie farm," "We lived in a sod house and I was privileged to ride the lead horse of the team which was opening the virgin soil."

With humor and at time poignancy, Hoover describes both the boyhood joys and the hard work and deprivations of this bucolic existence. A farm was "all kinds of factories," and every winter the cellar was full of stored food—"social security itself." Only 20 per cent of the farm produce was sold and consequently the effects of fluctuations on the Chicago market less felt. On the other hand, Hoover remembered, there was more sickness and death, and while food was abundant and clothing and shelter comfortable, there was but "little resource left for the other purposes of living."

For Henry A. Wallace, whose family was among the most prominent in Iowa, from the outset the problem was how to help farmers, not how personally to eke out a living on the land. Wallace, like his father and grandfather, who influenced him greatly, from the time he was very small was interested in plant science. As a six-year-old he was already being taken on walks through the fields and woods by that remarkable black scientist, George Washington Carver.

"It was he," Wallace wrote as vice president, "who first introduced me to the mysteries of plant fertilization . . . . Though I was a small boy he gave me credit for being able to identify different species of grasses . . . . Later on I was to have an intimate acquaintance with plants myself, because I spent a good many years breeding corn." Wallace's prime concerns were to be with the problems of the farmer and the improvement of the yield from Iowa's soil.

For young Harry Hopkins, whose family after much moving around and even a sojourn in Chicago, settled into Grinnell, there were apparently no comparable experiences. Yet fate almost sent Hopkins into a rural or small-town career rather than an urban one. Near the close of his senior year at Grinnell College, he toyed with the idea of running a newspaper in Bozeman, Montana, with Chester Davis, but in the end took a settlement house job in New York. Instead of Hopkins, Davis obtained another Grinnell man, Paul Appleby. (During the New Deal, Davis and Appleby were key administrators under Wallace in Washington.) For Hopkins, the transit from the abundance of nature in Iowa to the deprivation of the slums of New York was a shock. "He had certainly known poverty in his own family and friendly neighborhood in the Middle West, but that kind of poverty involved the maintenance of a kind of dignity and self-respect and independence," Robert Sherwood has written; "it did not involve hunger, or squalor, or degradation . . . something alien, shocking and enraging."

The common thread for all three men was the ample demonstration of abundance and the promise of even greater abundance from the Iowa soil—indeed from the soil of the entire nation. All three were remarkably to be involved with agriculture, and in differing degrees with the problem of getting food and clothing to the needy. That all three became involved so conspicuously with food can be considered more than coincidence; food is a material manifestation of humanitarianism. Their optimism and their extraordinary enterprise also have some common or similar grounding.

All three came from deeply religious antecedents. Hopkins' father is said to have been notable for his prowess in a bowling alley. His mother, who had been a school teacher, was a devout and active Methodist. Hopkins, according to his sister, broke off from a Grinnell girl with whom he had long gone steady "because she did not practice religion in the same narrow way as Harry had been brought up to do." Wallace's grandfather, who had a large influence upon him, had been a Presbyterian preacher and carried much of his religious teaching with him into his editing of *Wallaces' Farmer*. As Theodore Wilson has pointed out in his paper, Wallace as a young man became deeply involved in various types of mysticism. I do not interpret his move into mysticism as one away from progressivism. Rather, with him as with Hopkins, after the early religious tenets had faded into the background, the zeal to be of service to one's fellow man continued unabated.

Hoover too had been brought up strictly in a religious household. His parents were members of the Society of Friends; there was something of mysticism in it, and it was a way of life. Too, the community was largely Quaker. The influence, as with Hopkins, was largely on the part of his mother, who had been a school teacher and became a preacher traveling widely around the area. She was also active on behalf of prohibition. Hoover remembered being "parked for the day at the polls, where the women were massed in an effort to make the men vote themselves dry." In his comments on Quakerism in his memoirs, Hoover well epitomized its effects upon his later views:

> The reflex of religious individualism is necessarily also economic individualism. The Friends have always held strongly to education, thrift, and individual enterprise. In consequence of plain living and hard work poverty has never been their lot. So far as I know, no member has ever been in jail or on public relief. This is largely because they take care of each other.

From the few charming, witty, poignant pages that Hoover wrote about his boyhood in West Branch and surrounding areas, there emerges a theme common not only to Quakers and to small towns in Iowa but to most of pre-industrial America. That was a sense of community. When disaster struck, as it did young Hoover, who lost both his parents, the children were reared and their education basically provided. First of all, his parents had at least meager savings and insurance, their own social security system. Second, augmenting it were relatives who took in the children; in the case of Hoover's uncle Allen, weighed down with a heavy mortgage, guardians paid nominal board out of the orphans' inheritance. Living with relatives stretched the small legacies so far that Hoover had several hundred dollars, together with his own savings, to launch him on his studies at Stanford University. Although Hoover did not say so, it is important to keep in mind that if there had been no legacy and no relatives, the Quaker community would have helped out.

In West Branch a rudimentary, tacit social security system operated, as it did widely throughout pre-industrial America. Rexford G. Tugwell in his sensitive memoir of his youth, *The Light of Earlier Days*, noted the beneficent functioning of small towns in western New York. Tugwell commented too on the fact that the warm-hearted inhabitants who always assumed a responsibility toward their neighbors in later decades became outraged when distant governments took over or prescribed these previously volunteer functions. It was hard for people who had grown up in this system to accept the fact during the Great Depression that the need was too massive for the community or even the states to cope as they always had before, that Christian voluntarism would no longer sustain the needy. Yet many who had been active Progressives were reluctant in the 1930s to abandon voluntarism.

Throughout Iowa there was also a sense of mission toward those outside of the community. For Hoover's mother it was a religious mission that took her elsewhere, and for some of Hoover's relatives it was a Quaker concern for the welfare of the Indians. To this, too, Hoover was exposed. As a help to his mother, he was taken in by an uncle who was United States Indian agent to the Osage nation, and Hoover spent eight or nine months, together with cousins, playing with Indian children in Pawhuska, Indian Territory. When he was eleven and moved permanently to Oregon, his uncle there, among other pursuits a doctor, took Hoover with him on visits to patients. He would explode to Hoover over the neglect that had made them sick. "The vigor of his disgust was equaled only by his determination to take no payment from poor non-Quaker families whom he called 'white trash.' "

A sense of mission toward the unfortunate outside of the community always burned strongly in Hoover, as it did in Wallace. It was one of the key ingredients in the Social Justice movement. In the early 1900s social justice was not yet the paramount concern of either of them. Harry Hopkins, on the other hand, became totally involved. Perhaps the influence of his mother, who was a prime mover in her church's missionary society, may have had something to do with it. More likely, it was the inspiration of one of Hopkins' professors at Grinnell, Edward A. Steiner, who in his course on applied Christianity focused on the teachings of Tolstoy. Steiner sent Hopkins east to work in a settlement house summer camp. Hopkins seized the opportunity simply in order to see New York, but after only two months felt he had found his vocation, to try to improve the plight of the underprivileged. At first, Hopkins served a sort of apprenticeship, living at Christadora House while he worked for one of the foremost charitable organizations. It is almost belaboring the point to remind you that early settlement houses were trying to recreate the conditions of the ideal small American community within the great cities, and that charitable organizations like that for which Hopkins worked, the Association for Improving the Condition of the Poor, depending upon private philanthropy, were an urban variant on the sort of non-governmental voluntary system of aid that flourished in the small towns of Iowa and elsewhere.

What then if the voluntary system did not suffice? To what extent and under what circumstances should there be government intervention? The main path of both social and economic reformers through the Populist and Progressive eras had been one of voluntarism, but there were frequent forks toward governmental controls when voluntarism proved inadequate. Many Iowans had long favored prohibition. Individual farmers could not successfully cope with railroads, mortgage houses, and distant markets. A prosperous Republican businessman like Gilbert N. Haugen was being entirely consistent as a progressive congressman (Gilbert Fite points out) in standing for every bit of federal intervention that would help farmers—except the parcel post, which would give mail order houses an advantage over Iowa merchants. Three generations of Wallaces, the most powerful voice of the farmers, favored intervention with no apparent exceptions.

In 1939 Hopkins, at that time secretary of commerce, returned to Grinnell College and without benefit of ghost writers discoursed rather extemporaneously on government:

> I was around this town for many years, and I found that this town had a government . . . and I learned that there was a State Legislature. I did not know much about it. I heard they collected taxes. I used to hear rumors that the railroads owned the Legislature in the State of Iowa. I learned later it was true. I had the vaguest knowledge about government. The less government interfered with me around this town, the better I liked it. I didn't even like to have the College authorities interfere with me too much.

If Hopkins recalled his earlier attitude correctly, it was not much different from that of young Hoover. There is reason, however, to regard his remarks more as New Deal rhetoric than accurate reminiscence. Not only was Iowa enacting a substantial amount of progressive regulatory legislation when Hopkins was a student, but he took a famous government course with Professor Jesse Macy and could not have been ignorant of what was happening.

While one cannot be entirely certain, the attitudes of the three young men toward eastern big business and finance capitalism probably had much in common, and resembled the Iowa consensus. All three were the sons of entrepreneurs, of Iowa small businessmen serving the farm population. Hopkins' father, after many troubles, had established a harness store in Grinnell, and supplemented his lagging sales of harness by selling supplies to the college students. Jesse Hoover, starting as a blacksmith, was on his way up as a merchant of farm equipment when he died at the age of thirty-four. He was also an innovator, developing a pump for cattle troughs and a kind of barbed wire. The senior Wallaces, already excelling in agricultural experimentation, had established a successful farm paper. Through their editorials, all three of the Wallaces had inveighed against the rapacity of the eastern establishment.

Hoover's contemporary views are sketchy. Being older than Henry A. Wallace and Hopkins, he was well along in his career during the Progressive era, and through almost all of those years outside of the United States. We do know that he ardently admired Theodore Roosevelt, and indeed in 1912, at the dramatic zenith of the New Nationalism, contributed to Roosevelt's campaign fund. Subsequently, during World War I, he became the most famed lieutenant of Wilson, as witness Hoover's memoir, *The Ordeal of Woodrow Wilson*. Even in his old age, Hoover retained a good bit of the Iowa idiom of his boyhood. Once, referring to his troubles with Secretary of State Henry L. Stimson over Japan, he remarked, "Stimson thought economic sanctions *would cure chilblains*." There also remained a sprinkling of Iowa ideology. In the same conversation he referred darkly to the speculators and financiers of Wall Street—even though he himself at the time was seated comfortably in his suite in the tower of the Waldorf-Astoria Hotel.

There are other characteristics of these three men (or of two of them in some instances) that were of significance, although by no means limited to progressivism or Iowa. All three, while quite young, demonstrated outstanding leadership characteristics—Hoover in his legendary entrepreneurial career as a member of the first class at Stanford University, Hopkins winning election as permanent president of his class at Grinnell. Campus politics, though far removed from outside issues in those years, was, like moot court in law schools, preparation for later careers. Hoover developed early a keen mastery of public relations. Wallace at Iowa State, in contrast, was withdrawn and studious, deeply involved in plant genetics, but already influencing the outside world through his writing on agriculture. All three had organizing ability.

Wallace and Hoover both were of a scientific and mechanical bent. In keeping with the progressive emphasis upon "facts and figures" and scientific solutions to social problems, both were keenly interested in fact finding, statistics, and, upon the basis of these, planning. Before the war Hoover was applying his knowledge in the development of world mining enterprises; he was ready to bring an engineering or management solution to national and international problems.

Some scholars have regarded Hoover as something of a "technocrat." Both he and Wallace read the writings of the iconoclastic progressive social scientist Thorstein Veblen, whose ideas the technocrats later built upon. In 1911, David Burner notes, Hoover wrote an actress friend that he was constructing "a drama to represent to the world a new intellectual type from a literary or stage view—the modern intellectual engineer." Wallace actually met Veblen, who was teaching at the University of Missouri, at a midwestern conference and remembered that Veblen had with him Isador Lubin. Here again there was an intertwining, for Lubin was to be statistician for Hoover's Food Administration and later commissioner of labor statistics during the New Deal.

Wallace first put statistics to work to determine the cost factors in raising hogs and, consequently, the price farmers must receive to make a profit. Through the 1920s he explored one new area after another, determining cycles in livestock production and market prices, the effects of weather, and the tendency of families as incomes rose to have less children.

Hopkins was meanwhile moving in other directions, undergoing the apprenticeship that would prepare him for his role in the New Deal. It was in the social justice tradition, but was not the sort of experience he could have obtained in Iowa. He became expert as the executive director of the New York Tuberculosis Association, identifying new undertakings in which it should become involved, most notably the problem of silicosis. In combating disease and promoting public health, he transformed the association's $90,000 surplus into a $40,000 deficit, but in the prosperous twenties was skilled in raising far larger funds than the association had ever received before. Previously, it had conducted the sale of its famous Christmas seals in small lots at a penny apiece; Hopkins mailed them out in sheets of a hundred. In his fight for public health he became impatient with local and state restrictions, but was still operating within the bounds of voluntarism and private philanthropy.

Thus, already as young men, Hoover, Wallace, and Hopkins in their approach to problems all embodied numerous aspects of progressivism, much of it owing something to Iowa. I have purposely concentrated upon their background and formative years since these are less familiar. Their achievements (and also their shortcomings) as national leaders are so well known that I need only allude to them without detailed explanations.

The three Iowans brought with them onto the national scene numerous others of similar background. (Of course, through the Progressive era and later there were Iowans of national prominence in no way beholden to them, such as Representative Haugen, who gave his name to the McNary-Haugen farm plan. Wallace is inseparable from his father and grandfather, towering figures in national farm politics for decades.) It was Henry A. Wallace who brought Chester Davis and Paul Appleby to the AAA and Department of Agriculture.

Hoover appointed President Ray Lynman Wilbur of Stanford, born in Iowa, to be his secretary of the interior. Joseph F. Wall cites the finding of Kathryn Jagow Mohrman in his bicentennial history of Iowa that Hopkins made his alma mater, Grinnell, foremost among all small liberal arts colleges in the nation in its contribution of administrators to the New Deal. Hopkins appointed two women from among his classmates, Hallie Flanagan to direct the Federal Theatre Project, and Florence Kerr to head the Women's Division of the WPA.

The outstanding Iowan nationally, and the first to become famous, was Hoover. His resourceful organization and operation of the commission that kept millions of Belgians and French behind the German lines from starving during World War I made him a national hero. In 1917, after the United States entered the war, President Wilson appointed Hoover head of the Food Administration. Hoover undertook through profit incentives rather than coercion to channel farm production into commodities most needed for shipment to France, and to stimulate higher productivity. American food could help win the war and rescue millions from certain hunger and possible death. Similarly, he tried to persuade Americans to adjust their eating habits and to plant war gardens. Through "Hooverizing" Americans cut consumption of what the Allies needed without resort to rationing. At the outset, Hoover issued a press statement explaining why he was opposed to rationing and the fixing of retail prices:

> I hold that Democracy can yield to discipline and that we can solve this food problem for our own people and for our allies largely by voluntary action. To have done so will have been a greater service than our immediate objective, for we have demonstrated the rightness of our faith and our ability to defend ourselves without being Prussianized.

In the aftermath of the war, with much of central and eastern Europe facing incipient starvation and Communist revolution, Hoover transformed the Food Administration into a government agency for overseas relief. It was the great forerunner of the relief programs of World War II and the foreign aid programs since. To Hoover it was in part the means of trying to stem the tide of revolution, but above all it was simply the humanitarianism that had become part of his fiber in growing up. He fought against the blockading of food for the Germans, and in 1921 came under criticism for sending aid to Soviet Russia. Hoover retorted, "Twenty million people are starving. Whatever their politics, they shall be fed."

Hoover was such an international hero that he was able to specify the terms under which he entered President Harding's cabinet in 1921. He became secretary of commerce, but with the right to be involved in other areas as well. He came to have so many interests that one can best epitomize them by referring to a famous cartoon, "The Traffic Problem in Washington," by J. N.

"Ding" Darling of the *Des Moines Register*. It shows President Coolidge as a traffic cop halting cars while a whole procession of Hoovers, each wearing a different label in his hat, comes striding across the street. Actually, Coolidge's view of Hoover's wide-ranging dynamism was less than enthusiastic. He remarked once in private that his secretary of commerce was "nosy."

Secretary Hoover was the dominant administrator in New Era Washington, trying to help small business compete successfully with large, and to bring greater prosperity through standardization and efficiency. Ellis Hawley and others have been interested in analyzing and explaining this benign association between government and business. It combined organizational and technical skills with faith in individualism and abhorrence of government coercion.

For depressed agriculture, Hoover favored farm marketing and credit arrangements. Secretary Henry C. Wallace accepted these, but wanted something more, a price support program through the mechanism of the McNary-Haugen plan. That scheme was as unacceptable to Hoover as it was to President Coolidge, and there was a bitter struggle in the cabinet between the two secretaries. Young Henry A. Wallace, editing the family paper, gave strong support to his father. (The scheme, it might be noted, which would maintain an artificially high price within the United States while shipping surpluses abroad, seemed to draw more upon the realities of Hoover's Food Administration than of the Progressive era.)

Hoover, hailed as the "Great Engineer," demonstrated countless ways through which government could aid business. He was elected enthusiastically in 1928 as a president who could bring an ever-increasing prosperity, but it was his misfortune to become a depression president. He reacted far more vigorously than any of his predecessors in time of economic distress. Already in 1929, to try to raise lagging farm prices, he had obtained legislation to create the Federal Farm Board to buy up some of the agricultural surpluses. Like most of Hoover's subsequent measures, it was inadequate to meet the appalling challenge of the depression, yet made a positive contribution through setting up the machinery which made it possible for Henry A. Wallace's AAA to begin functioning at top speed in the summer of 1933. In other areas, too, Hoover created machinery which the New Deal could take over, usually modify, and put to its own uses.

In his fight against the depression, Hoover seemed at the time a bold innovator, utilizing to the full the progressive tradition and the approach with which he had been so successful as secretary of commerce. He continued to stress individualism and voluntarism in dealing with distressed businessmen, workers, farmers, and the needy. He continued, too, to fear overcentralization in Washington, the assumption of tasks that inherently belonged to the community or the state. He continued on what had been the main path of progressivism, avoiding as far as possible any governmental coercion.

The sheer massiveness of the national catastrophe made Hoover's approach inadequate. The depression was so deep that private charities, the communities, and the states could not meet the needs as they always had before. Voluntarism no longer sufficed. Large manufacturers of durable goods could cut back, but competitive producers of textiles, petroleum, and bituminous coal could not do so without courting bankruptcy. Farmers on the brink of disaster could not heed Hoover's plea to plant less.

So it was that Hoover's program for fighting the depression gave way to that of Roosevelt. The emphasis upon voluntarism was still there, but behind the language of voluntarism there were to be found economic incentives (or in the case of the NRA even criminal penalties). This was the New Deal, in which Wallace and Hopkins played such a conspicuous part.

Secretary Wallace was a key figure in developing a more viable crop control program than McNary-Haugenism. At first through the device of a processing tax, later through soil conservation provisions, it reduced acreage of major crops and subsidized farmers who complied. National planning in the area of agriculture became accepted federal policy. Wallace also became interested in numerous programs, difficult to obtain from Congress, to aid marginal farmers and sharecroppers. His scientific interests continued unabated; it was he, for instance, who modernized the Weather Bureau.

Wallace, who had always stood for an agriculture of abundance, and who had done much to make higher crop yields a reality through hybrid corn, seemed to be in an incongruous position presiding over crop limitations. His rationale was that controls would bring higher farm prices; these in turn would contribute to national prosperity. Then, with consumer buying power restored, full production could return, and even storage could be implemented through an "ever normal granary" plan as a safeguard against famine years. (Wallace enjoyed telling that the granary plan was an ancient Chinese idea he had learned about in the Des Moines public library.) Meanwhile, during the years when it was necessary to reduce crops, Wallace was channeling surplus toward the needy. Pork and cotton went at once in 1933; before the end of the thirties there were food stamps, with which those on Hopkins' relief rolls could purchase commodities in oversupply.

During and immediately after World War II, farmers again were exhorted to produce to the utmost to feed the world. Wallace and Hopkins were both involved, at least indirectly. After VJ Day it was Hoover who appraised the world needs for food to avert famine, acting on behalf of President Harry S. Truman. Once again he was engaged in humanitarian planning. The American granary barely sufficed to prevent widespread starvation, but suffice it did.

In the New Deal years, Harry Hopkins served, as Searle F. Charles has entitled his monograph, as *Minister of Relief*. He did not abandon his early ideals of individual self-reliance. He wanted programs like the Civil Works Administration to last only long enough to keep the unemployed from going hungry. He insisted upon work relief to prevent workers' skills from becoming rusty, their morale from eroding, and because he firmly believed that people should work for what they got.

Although Hopkins came under attack because of alleged corruption and waste in the federal relief program, the amazing thing is that he supervised the expenditure of some $9 billion, a staggering sum in the 1930s, with no more than minor scandals. Most of the trouble came at the local and state levels. Hopkins forthrightly held that what could not be achieved there must be undertaken by the federal government. In his talk at Grinnell College in 1939, after exaggerating his undergraduate parochialism, he went on to say:

> I have lived to see the time when the Government of the United States worries about how much a farmer gets for his corn, wheat, or cotton. I have lived to see the time when a farmer gets a check signed by the Treasurer of the United States for doing something. I see old people getting pensions; see unemployed people getting checks from the United States Goverment; college students getting checks signed by the United States Government.

To Hopkins there was nothing improper about any of this; he insisted it was equally right in a democracy for various groups to struggle for control of the government. The point he was trying to make to the students was that they should regard the government as theirs, and that with their brains and skill they should be involved with it.

The purport of the extensive New Deal involvement in the economy and society was quite different to ex-President Hoover. The concerns of Hopkins, Wallace, and the many others to him marked a disastrous abandonment of what he had considered fundamental. Joan Hoff Wilson demonstrates in her paper on Hoover's criticisms of the New Deal that his strictures were in keeping with progressive traditions. An array of one-time Progressives, as Otis Graham has shown, shared Hoover's views.

Does that mean, then, that Wallace and Hopkins were traitors to the Iowa progressivism in which they had been nurtured? I think not. It is true that the New Deal in many respects went well beyond progressivism, but it is also true that it was a logical outgrowth. Even during the Progressive era there had been many who found the main course of voluntarism would not work and branched off toward governmental controls. Indeed, as the movement had gone on, it had involved more and more federal legislation and regulation. Whether or not it was desirable is still a matter of debate; certainly it was logical.

The conflicts between the advocates of Hoover's view on the one hand and those of Wallace and Hopkins on the other continue to be heated, and rightfully so. The origins are similar, but the distinctions sharp. I have not intended this paper to be an exercise in consensus history. The quest goes on for an ideal balance between freedom and regulation. While we engage in that search and continue to debate where the point of balance should be set, we can all hail the achievements of each of these three forward-looking, creative leaders, who each in his own way contributed to a better America and world.

APPENDIX

GILBERT NELSON HAUGEN was born on April 21, 1859, in Rock County, Wisconsin, the son of Norwegian immigrants. At age fourteen he moved with his family to Decorah, Iowa, and at eighteen he purchased a farm in Worth County, making his home in Northwood. In 1885 he married Berthe Elise Evensen; they had two children, Lauritz and Norma. By 1890 he had expanded his land holdings, established an implement and livestock business in Kinsett, and become the president of the Northwood Banking Company.

After serving three terms as county treasurer (1887-1893) and two as state representative (1894-98), he became the Republican nominee for Congress in 1898. He was elected and served Iowa's Fourth District for seventeen successive terms (1899-1933). He was a member of the House Committee on Agriculture from 1899 to 1933 and its chairman from 1919 to 1931. He was defeated in the 1932 elections and died in Northwood July 18, 1933.

Born in West Branch, Iowa, on August 10, 1874, HERBERT CLARK HOOVER was orphaned at nine and lived with an uncle in Oregon from the age of eleven until he was seventeen. He graduated from Stanford University in May, 1895, and began a career in international mining engineering which, by 1910, was to bring him interests and chairmanships in several mining companies as well as a worldwide reputation in his field. He married Lou Henry in 1899. They had two children, Herbert and Allan Henry.

Based in London at the outbreak of World War I, Hoover organized the American Relief Committee, which assisted 120,000 Americans in getting home from Europe. During the next four years he organized and directed the Commission for Relief in Belgium, which fed some ten million civilians in German-occupied Belgium and northern France. He also served as U.S. food administrator (1917-19) and headed several organizations aimed at averting famine in postwar Europe. His effort to obtain the 1920 Republican presidential nomination failed, but in 1921 President Harding appointed him secretary of commerce, a post he held for seven years. He was elected president by a wide margin in 1928 and took office eight months before the stock market crashed. Despite such countermeasures as the Reconstruction Finance Corporation, the depression deepened and Hoover was soundly defeated in the 1932 presidential election.

After leaving the presidency, Hoover moved from Palo Alto to New York City and spent much time speaking and writing about public affairs. After World War II he served as chairman of the Famine Emergency Commission, a post in which he studied world food needs and recommended steps to fill them. In 1947 he became chairman of the Commission on Organization of the Executive Branch of the Government (also called the Hoover Commission), whose adopted proposals streamlined the government and cut federal costs. Hoover died in New York City October 20, 1964.

HENRY AGARD WALLACE was born in Adair County, Iowa, on October 7, 1888. After graduating from Iowa State College in 1910, he became associate editor of *Wallaces' Farmer*. He married Ilo Brown in 1914; they had three children: Henry B., Robert, and Jean. He succeeded his father as editor in 1921 and remained in that post until 1933, meanwhile developing high-yielding strains of corn, which he marketed through his own firm, the Pioneer Hi-Bred Corn Company.

Wallace served as secretary of agriculture during Franklin D. Roosevelt's first two terms (1933-1941), speaking out strongly for New Deal measures and setting up the Agricultural Adjustment Administration. He served as vice president during Roosevelt's third term (1941-45), but was denied renomination in the Democratic convention of 1944. He served as secretary of commerce in 1945-46.

In 1948 his disagreement with Truman administration policies toward the Soviet Union helped lead him to accept the presidential nomination of the newly-formed Progressive party. He left the party in 1950, after it repudiated his endorsement of U.S.-UN action in Korea, and resumed his activity with Pioneer from his farm in upstate New York. He died in Danbury, Connecticut, November 18, 1965.